YOU'RE ALREADY A WEALTH HEIRESS!

Now Think and Act Like One

6 PRACTICAL STEPS TO MAKE IT A REALITY NOW

LINDA P. JONES

Post Hill
PRESS

A POST HILL PRESS BOOK

ISBN: 978-1-68261-645-1
ISBN (eBook): 978-1-68261-646-8

Post Hill Press, LLC
New York • Nashville
posthillpress.com

Published in the United States of America

This book is dedicated to my sister Marilyn, who has always been there for me; my late husband, Roger, who gave me the happiest years of my life; and my parents, Leonard and Arline Penitsch, whom I adore and miss every day. You made me who I am today and taught me how to be an investor and wealth builder.

CONTENTS

Wealth Heiress 101

Chapter 1: You Are a Wealth Heiress..............................7
Chapter 2: The Inspiring Stories of Wealth Heiresses..................20
Chapter 3: The Nature of Bubbles and Cycles 29
Chapter 4: Why Calculated Risk Is a Good Thing.......................39
Chapter 5: The Six Steps to Wealth 50

The Six Steps to Wealth

Chapter 6: Step One: Create a Wealthy Mindset 65
Chapter 7: Step Two: Build a Nest Egg...75
Chapter 8: Smart and Not-So-Smart Spending............................89
Chapter 9: Good Debt and Bad Debt 97
Chapter 10: Step Three: Find a Mentor and Get Knowledgeable 105
Chapter 11: Step Four: Invest in a Money Engine 113
Chapter 12: Step Five: Compound at a High Rate 122
Chapter 13: Step Six: Protect Your Wealth 127

Embracing Individual Challenges

Chapter 14: What If You Do Not Have Enough Time
          in Your Day?...135
Chapter 15: What If You Do Not Have an Interest in Financial
          Matters? 139
Chapter 16: What If Your Spouse, Partner,
          or Family is an Obstacle? 144

Chapter 17: What If You Are a Millennial, Gen-Xer, or Baby
      Boomer? 148

Your Personal Plan

Chapter 18: The Wealth Building Formula™ 159
Chapter 19: Your Own Millionaire Action Plan (MAP)™ 166
Chapter 20: Now Go Do It! 185

Resources 191
Endnotes...193
Acknowledgments 203
About the Author..205

WEALTH
HEIRESS 101

CHAPTER 1

You Are a Wealth Heiress

"Your Wealth Heiress is the smart, capable,
confident, successful, and wealthy woman already
inside of you who has yet to be fully discovered."

You have inherited an unrealized, potential financial genius that lies inside you. I call her your Wealth Heiress. You have probably never heard about her before, but I assure you that she is there just waiting for you to take action and bring her into reality.

I will show you—without a doubt—why this is true. You will learn what, why, and how to realize your inner Wealth Heiress.

You will find the ability to realize your financial dreams and create, grow, and manage wealth. It is not only possible; it is realistic. I believe if you have the right knowledge and make the right choices, then you can become wealthy, no matter how much or little you are starting with.

You will discover practical tips and wealth concepts to understand exactly how to create wealth as well as connect your mindset with the core principles and actions for you to realize your Wealth Heiress.

This book is not about the dry, boring side of money. It is not recycled information you have heard over and over, nor is it traditional advice that you get from a financial advisor. Neither you nor I care to hear the same old stuff.

Too often financial information for women has been about FICO scores or managing debt instead of addressing what is really holding many of you back—not being *interested* in financial matters. Whether this is your first or one hundredth financial book, I congratulate you for taking positive action to change your life. It is my intention to interest women who have not been interested in financial matters before and to encourage those who have. These principles work for men too; it is just written with the special struggles women have in mind.

You will learn the answer to a burning question I have had all my life: Why are some people rich, and how did they get that way? And fortunately, I am going to spare you the suggestions of things to do to become a millionaire that I have read such as make your bed (I kid you not), read lots of books no matter what kind, exercise, meditate, budget with a spreadsheet, live in a house the size of a shed, ride a bike instead of owning a car, and other ridiculous notions on how to become wealthy.

Wealth and Women

I strongly believe that women have unique challenges, but some blessings are coming their way too. For example, there is a phenomenal shift happening that shows that we are actually holding a lot of really good cards in our hand. Over the next decade, women will control two-thirds of consumer wealth in the U.S. and be the beneficiaries of the largest transference of wealth in our country's history. Estimates range from twelve to forty trillion dollars.[1]

Additionally, the number of wealthy women investors in the United States is growing at a faster rate than that of men. In a two-year period, the number of wealthy women in the United States grew 68 percent, while the number of wealthy men grew only 36 percent.[2]

And a statistic that truly brings joy to my heart: According to a Fidelity Investments 2017 report, a twenty-two-year-old female investor starting out with a salary of $50,000 a year will outpace her male counterpart by more than $250,000.[3]

With this kind of wealth coming, it is imperative that we have a handle on understanding wealth principles. I think it is more important than ever for women to develop the confidence of their Wealth Heiress so they can be good stewards of money.

There is also a frightening statistic: The majority of women are entering old age in poverty.[4] I see three reasons why this is happening. First, middle-aged women have earned less than men over their careers and are starting behind the curve. Second, many women have not taken an interest in financial matters, whether they are fine delegating it, or are overburdened with work and family obligations, or find it boring. And third is the trend of having a "celebrity closet" where women are encouraged to pack their closets full of expensive shoes, handbags, and clothes that they rarely use. It is causing women to focus on things that don't build them wealth. It is time to reverse the trends and give women the knowledge and tools they need to excel financially if they aren't already.

I have spent my life researching how wealth grows. I can show you what works because I did it myself, making $2 million by age thirty-nine. It is my passion to share this knowledge as America's Wealth Mentor™ on the *Be Wealthy & Smart* podcast, an internet radio show on iTunes that is broadcast in 171 countries with over 1.5 million downloads. As Benjamin Disraeli said: "The greatest good you can do for another is not just to share your riches, but to reveal to him his own."[5]

Contrary to what some experts espouse, wealth is not about being miserly and saving your way to wealth, couponing, or winning the lottery. It is not about marrying rich. It is not about being born into a wealthy family. It is not about luck. I want you to know right now that the ability to achieve your financial dreams already lies within you. I have seen it time and time again.

Like the fifty-year-old female professional who turned a $100,000 inheritance into $1 million; the forty-five-year-old widow who became a multimillionaire when she took over her investment portfolio from her late husband's broker; or the thirty-five-year-old mother who turned a small side business into a real-estate portfolio, combining two powerful money engines.

These are just a sampling of women who inspire me. What does each have in common? They are ordinary women who became extraordinary. Their age did not matter. Their social status did not matter. Their ethnic backgrounds did not matter. Most importantly, their gender did not matter. Each woman developed her inner Wealth Heiress by learning, thinking, and acting like one.

They followed a process I call the Six Steps to Wealth, which is how many people become wealthy. I developed the steps after recognizing many millionaires have taken them. I'll share with you the Wealth Building Formula, which explains the vital connection between money, compounding, and time. I created this formula to help make wealth building simple. You will also be given a plan of action to become rich—your Millionaire Action Plan (MAP)™, a strategic process that shows you exactly what to do to reach a million dollars and how to overcome any obstacles you face to reach that goal. Each of these tools will be revealed in depth with you in upcoming chapters.

What Stops Women

So what stops women from activating her Wealth Heiress? The biggest factor I have seen is a lack of confidence that they can do it, so they don't even try. In some instances, I have even talked with women who felt they were not worthy and deserving of wealth. How sad is that?

This lack of confidence is epidemic. Many women do not see how wonderful they are. Society mandates that women think of others and not ourselves. We support others and help them be successful, but what about our own success? Is it wrong for women to pursue their own success? Absolutely not. In fact, it is imperative that women achieve financial success so that they can have a multiplying effect and make a difference in the world.

Another thing that stops women is a lack of interest in financial matters. Women tell me they know the family investments are something they *should* know about but are frankly not interested in. Finance is almost a foreign language that is often intimidating and just not fun for many women. They see it as boring, like watching

ESPN all day if you are not a sports lover. It makes their eyes roll back in their heads. That is one of my inspirations for writing this book: to present financial matters in a way that women like.

Many years ago, I gave a seminar to women based on a book a man wrote about women and money. Afterwards, a woman asked me, "Why didn't *you* write the book?" Her question caught me off guard. I could have written that book, but I didn't.

The truth is, at that point in my life, I did not see the different needs women had in regard to learning about investing. Working on Wall Street, we talked to men and women with the same jargon and boring statistics. It was only after leaving Wall Street, starting my business, and working with hundreds of women that I realized the financial industry was not addressing all of their needs or interests. The boardrooms of Wall Street firms were not fully aware of what women want, need, or how to make them feel comfortable.

It is about meeting women where they are and giving them the confidence and knowledge that they can do it. It is treating them with respect. It is listening to what matters to them and what they value because the goals of husbands and wives can be very different even though they reside in the same family. It is presenting the information in a way that interests and inspires them, rather than spouting columns of numbers and financial lingo.

We are not talking about the effect these attitudes and practices have on just a few women. We are talking about the majority. Here are two very telling survey results. Eighty-seven percent of women feel misunderstood by investment experts, and 70 percent leave the family financial advisor within one year after their husbands die.[6]

Women are realizing they need control over finances, and the only way to do that is to become actively involved in wealth creation. They realize they cannot sit passively by and let others—fathers, husbands, or financial advisors—make decisions for them.

And please understand this: Wealth is possible for you, but if you do not take action, then you will not succeed. This will be just another advice book sitting on your shelf. I do not want this to happen. I want you to become wealthy. It is within your power, and that is why this book is written with specific steps for you to take action.

Debunking Myths about Wealth Building

There are many myths that have limited wealth creation among both men and women. We have been told so much about wealth building that is simply not true. One of the purposes of this book is to debunk these myths. Here are some common myths that hold women back from believing they can achieve wealth:

- *The myth that wealth building is too difficult.* The belief that wealth building is too hard and not within your reach is bogus. It is a matter of financial education and putting good habits into practice. I believe if you make the right choices and avoid common financial mistakes, it is possible to become wealthy.
- *The myth that what you believe about money does not matter.* One of the most important things that is left out of almost all financial training is the importance of your thoughts and beliefs about wealth and wealthy people. What beliefs—good and bad—have you internalized that parents, society, and stereotypes taught you about wealth and wealthy people? One client told me her father always cursed the rich man down the street. She did not know why but realized she internalized the belief all rich people are bad. If you subconsciously view all wealthy people as bad or cheating crooks, will you want to be wealthy, or will you self-sabotage?
- *The myth that being wealthy means unlimited spending.* One reason why lottery winners go broke is they only know how to spend, not create, money. If you only understand spending, do not know how to create more money, and believe money is something that is *only spent*, then you will tend to spend until it is all gone. When you become wealthy, if you do not understand wealth management and how to create more by investing, you will likely run out. Sound familiar? Think Johnny Depp, Toni Braxton, Janice Dickinson, M.C. Hammer, Kim Basinger, and Mike Tyson.

- *The myth of frugality.* A popular belief today is you must be a miser and save as much money as possible to become wealthy. This is what I call the "frugalist" movement. People somehow think if they scrimp and save enough, they can become wealthy. That is not possible for most people. You cannot starve your way to wealth. You can only cut so many expenses before you are living in the woods! There is the rare exception of the high-paid tech worker who squirrels away quite a bit of his or her multiple six-figure salary and gets to $1,000,000, but for most people, it is impossible to simply save your way to wealth. *There must be an investing component to grow your money and get it to begin compounding for you.* Many stories I have read about people saving money and becoming millionaires oddly omit the part where they compounded their money at a high rate. Compounding is how money grows and multiplies over time. Your money grows, and the money it creates grows too.

- *The myth that debt is always bad.* There's also a popular belief that all debt is bad and that you should pay it off early—including mortgage debt. I am a fan of debt when you use it to build appreciating assets such as real estate, a business, go to college, or invest in anything that can increase in value. Using other people's money (OPM) is a common proven strategy of many millionaires. However, I do shun consumer debt. Borrowing to buy designer clothing, meals at expensive restaurants, brand new vehicles, and other depreciating items is not a good reason to incur debt.

- *The myth that budgets are necessary to build wealth.* Another common misconception is that you must be on a budget to build wealth. In my opinion, budgets can be hazardous to your wealth because they feel restrictive. Like a diet, you want to go off a budget as soon as you start. Instead, I will show you how to *prioritize your spending* on the things that are important to you so you do not end up feeling deprived and go on an unplanned shopping spree or develop a bad relationship with money. There is one exception. If you are deeply in debt or barely make enough income to pay your bills, then a budget is *absolutely necessary* to keep you disciplined with every dollar until your debt is paid off.

- **The myth that good investing focuses on the past.** Many investors mistakenly look in the rearview mirror to make investment decisions. Looking in the past causes them to invest in the wrong place at the wrong time such as buying a tech mutual fund in 2000 or buying a home at the peak of a bubble. Using cycle information gives you a roadmap and prevents you from making horrible mistakes that set back your wealth building and can even delay your retirement. Cycles are a secret that only a few in the investment community acknowledge and understand. I will talk about them extensively in chapter 3.

How I Learned These Truths

I grew up in a middle-class home on Mercer Island, an island that is a suburb of Seattle, where many wealthy people live. Paul Allen, cofounder of Microsoft, is one of them. Curiosity about how to become wealthy motivated me to read biographies of millionaires and study wealth building even as a child. I read *Think and Grow Rich* when I was ten years old.

As a young person, I was already noticing the differences between my modest upbringing and my wealthy friends. I wanted to have a lot of money, too. Not because I loved money so much, but because I understood that if you wanted to live a full life, a life without limits, a life of freedom to do what you wanted, it would take a lot of money. I wanted to experience everything and not be restricted by a lack of money. I dreamed of traveling all over the world, having a nice home and nice things.

Not everyone has a great role model, but I was fortunate that my mom loved to invest. By the time I came along after my two brothers and two sisters, my mom was a housewife who also invested in real estate with my dad. He worked full-time as an industrial engineer at Boeing, but in their spare time, they invested in rental houses, apartment buildings, and a warehouse.

On a pretty small salary, they managed to raise five kids, put them through college, and invest in property. Mom could sure find sales and stretch dollars. I learned by observing them, and the most important lesson I learned is this: *If you want to be financially secure in life, you have to take your income and turn it into investments.*

As a child, I had to earn my allowance. Sometimes that meant working for hire at the twenty-five-unit apartment building my parents owned on Mercer Island. We had a manager who rented apartments, but when a tenant moved out, my brothers and sisters and I would clean and paint the apartment for the next tenant. We were paid hourly, and we learned a lot about hard work.

My fascination with how wealth is created made me study everything about money and investing, get a job with a Wall Street investment firm, and start investing for myself. There were many wrong turns and some failures. In fact, the first investment I made was in a mutual fund that almost immediately declined by 30 percent. No one told me the investment that goes up the fastest would also drop the fastest when the stock market declines; hence, I invested at exactly the top before a big market drop.

Besides mutual funds, I also invested in real estate and eventually in individual stocks. Over time, I was able to improve and create more successes, which meant compounding my money faster.

I think having a "big why" is helpful for women because we're often not motivated by money itself. It is the "why" behind the money that drives us. Perhaps it is paying for our children's college, taking a nice vacation, or saving for a nicer home.

Connecting to your big why can make building wealth much more personal and meaningful to you than a goal of $1 million. Why is it you want the money? What will you do with it? Some women have told me they do not feel motivated by money, so having a reason or plan for the money can make a big difference to help motivate you to take action.

The motivation for more money in my case involved tapping into a desire I had to become a mom and be able to afford a nanny. Since I was the main breadwinner, I reasoned that if I wanted a family, I'd have to hire someone to take care of the baby.

As it turned out, $2 million came, but the baby did not. I was not able to have children, so eventually my plans changed. My husband and I ended up taking a small portion of the money to have a large party, travel on luxury cruise lines to exotic locations, and add to our art collection. They were incredibly fun years. But then life threw me a vicious curveball.

On the night of December 13, 2005, my husband and I were home alone when he suddenly collapsed, unconscious and not breathing. I gave him CPR and called 911. The medics arrived, shot needles with adrenaline into his heart, and worked on him for twenty minutes. He was not responding and was turning blue. Time was running out, and I couldn't accept that my husband could die. I prayed out loud, just the four medics and me. Immediately, I heard a medic say, "We have a heartbeat." Off we raced to the hospital.

I was hopeful Roger would recover, but it was not meant to be. Although we guessed it was a heart attack, the hospital said it was a brain aneurysm. Roger had no headache or warning at all. He was in intensive care for two weeks and never regained consciousness. The doctors said he had less than a one percent chance of a full recovery. Surrounded by family on December 27, we removed him from the respirator, and he died immediately.

One minute my husband was alive, and the next he was not. I kept thinking it was a bad dream, but it was real. I was grieving, having panic attacks, and I couldn't remember simple things like my home address. I had things to do, bequests to make, and an account-ing of our assets and papers to sign. Working with the lawyers to close probate was a pretty awful experience. My husband was not even dead for forty-eight hours when my new lawyer met me and said, "You are young. You will remarry."

I was treated not as the investment professional I was but as if I knew nothing. Billing their time at over $300 an hour, costs added up fast. Fortunately, because of my knowledge, I caught a mistake my law-yer made. I would have owed $50,000 in estate taxes had I not caught it. Two years later, I was relieved when probate was finally closed.

I had enough money to be able to retire, and after much soul searching, I decided to leave Wall Street and start a business as a wealth mentor. The Global Institute of Wealth for Women™ was born.

Today my personal goals are to have a company that goes public and trades on the stock exchange. I'd love to speak at Madison Square Garden. I would also love to have my own foundation that donates money to women in need. I'd love to do more traveling, host parties and charitable events, and spend time on a ranch with a lake where I grow my own fruits and vegetables.

I am telling you this to show you I was already the woman I needed to be to realize my Wealth Heiress. She was inside me all along. I just had to gain knowledge, get rid of my fears, and step completely outside of my comfort zone.

My Wealth Heiress continues to make new goals, so the goals I just shared with you are those I am striving for today because your Wealth Heiress is always evolving and progressing. Your Wealth Heiress wants you to continue to better yourself, set new goals, and reach new heights of success.

Will You Choose to Develop Your Potential?

A tree seed will grow when planted and watered, and the potential for a large, glorious tree already exists within the seed. It is a law of nature. You also have inherited the potential to realize your inner Wealth Heiress—a confident woman with success and wealth. Now it is up to you to add the water that creates the beautiful tree—the decisions, determination, and actions to become a millionaire.

Your life is what you make it. It is up to you what you do with it. Are you holding yourself back and letting your seed of potential lie dormant or are you developing it into a beautiful, flowering tree that creates an abundance of seeds and your beautiful Wealth Heiress?

I think when our life is over and we reach the pearly gates, we may have to account for how much or how little of our potential or talents we used. I imagine a conversation with God that goes like this:

Person: Hello, God.
God: *Hello. Tell me about your life and why you chose the life you did.*
Person: What do you mean? I lived the life You gave me.
God: *I would have given you anything you believed you could be, do, or have. Why did you choose so little?*

Why indeed do some people choose so little? Why not go for it with gusto and reach for the stars? The decision is ours. Far too often, we do not try. We accept less than we should and do not realize the full splendor of our Wealth Heiress. Of course, we have doubts and uncertainty. Maybe we even lack confidence, but that has not stopped some women from having a big vision and working to make it happen. How did they do it? Are they geniuses? Born under a lucky star? Or have some magical advantage?

No. Women achieve wealth when they gain knowledge, plan, work hard, and take action. Like a GPS tracker, they course-correct when they lose their way. Examples of women who have achieved world-changing success provide a beacon for all of us as we activate our own Wealth Heiress. Women who have especially inspired me include Oprah Winfrey, Sara Blakely, J.K. Rowling, Coco Chanel, Jennifer Lopez, Arianna Huffington, Judith R. Faulkner, Debbi Fields, and Zhou Qunfei. I will tell you their stories in the next chapter.

I will also share stories of successful women entrepreneurs who are everyday people that have been able to create wealth. What they all have in common is they went for their dreams, took calculated risks, and developed their inner Wealth Heiress. Remember, she was within them all along. So is yours. She's just waiting for you to believe in her and take action.

Women can be fabulous investors. For instance, take these three pioneer women who started investing back in the 1960s, when most women did not work outside the home. Geraldine Weiss started with $2,000 that she grew into millions earning 11.22 percent over thirty years by investing in dividend-paying stocks such as Coca-Cola and PepsiCo.[7] Anne Scheiber, an IRS auditor, never earned more than $3,150 a year but learned from auditing tax returns that stocks created wealth. She turned a $5,000 investment into $22 million by owning stocks for fifty-one years until her death at age 101.[8] Muriel "Mickie" Siebert was the first woman to own a seat on the New York Stock Exchange in 1967. Today, her company contains assets under management of more than $11 billion.[9]

In short, it is possible for any woman to become wealthy. Especially you. The starting point is what we believe—our mindset, which I will be talking about extensively in chapter 6. I will show you that the more *certain* you are about your Wealth Heiress reaching the mental picture of your finish line, the more likely your vision will come true.

We all start our lives as young women dreaming of what's possible and wondering what we might accomplish with our lives. There's the longing to be the woman you always wanted to be. She might seem off in the distance, but she's not. She's right there within you.

What are your goals? What makes you tick? What secret desires do you have that might seem out of the ordinary? Because it is all okay. All of it. It is okay to dream and dream *big*. It is okay to be the fullest version of yourself.

Because I promise you, you *can* achieve everything you want to. It does not take super powers. You do not have to be Wonder Woman. You do not have to be extra talented or smart or lucky. You have to have determination, certainty, and confidence. You've got this.

The Bottom Line

It is up to you to unlock your wealth potential. My hope is that this book lights a fire in you to become interested in financial matters because women have a tsunami of either good or bad circumstances coming at them. It is up to *you* to decide which result you are going to have and whether your Wealth Heiress is realized.

Activate Your Wealth Heiress

1. Start a Wealth Heiress journal. It is vital that you write things down in this journal and refer to it every day. Here's your first assignment: Think about the ideal woman you wish you could be. Write down a one-paragraph description of her.
2. Spend three minutes visualizing your Wealth Heiress with your eyes closed. Do this nightly before going to sleep.

CHAPTER 2

The Inspiring Stories of Wealth Heiresses

*"Your Wealth Heiress lies within. It is up
to you to take action and make her a reality."*

Many famous Wealth Heiresses started out just like you and me. Some of these women had very humble beginnings. They were not born into a privileged life. They had hardships, challenges, and failures. Things did not go perfectly, and they certainly did not have overnight success. No, they started just like we did—unsure, unconfident, and, in most cases, underfunded; yet they were able to realize their Wealth Heiress.

The women we will be showcasing in this chapter did not start out as the people they are today. They had to grow into it. They had to study, improve, take action, and course-correct. They had to take risks and build the plane as they were flying it. They had twists and turns where they could have been bucked off the bronco if not for their fortitude.

They got stronger and more confident. They found their way and the finish line of their vision for success. They did not require brain transplants; they developed the abilities they were given. The Wealth Heiresses they became were *within them all along*. They activated something that was already there from birth. Your potential Wealth Heiress is there inside you too.

The biggest difference is they went after their dreams and developed certainty that they could achieve them. Many of us do not even try to achieve our dreams or even perhaps know what our dreams are. We put our own glass ceiling above us and think we cannot rise above it. We can. You can.

What's stopping you is fear—For Ever Alternate Reality (FEAR). The alternate reality where perhaps lack of certainty fuels doubt, negativity, and, eventually, quitting. We can be afraid of moving outside of our comfort zones, being criticized, putting ourselves out there, failure, and maybe even being seen. For some, there is too much risk of failure, and it results in never even trying—and perhaps worse, never finding your life's purpose.

There are a lot of fears we believe are real because it can be really frightening to step outside of the box, away from the crowd, and out of our comfort zone into the scary place that is the great unknown. When it is outside of our control, it can seem the scariest.

To develop your Wealth Heiress and all that she embodies, you have to go after your dreams, take your power, and grab the brass ring. It will not come knocking on your door. You have to take the taxi to the subway, the subway to the train, the train to the plane, and the plane to the rocket ship.

There's no direct path. There's no perfect way. There's no plan without mistakes, failure, and course-correction. The way to do it is to set your course on your vision of your Wealth Heiress and meet her halfway. She will do the rest of the work if you do not give up.

You may have a hard time believing that inside of you already exists this amazing woman. You may be afraid to take action. Often as women, we are taught to wait, not take risks, be polite, and maybe even be passive. Ladies are supposed to sit quietly and be seen and not heard, right? Forget that!

One of the most powerful ways to activate your Wealth Heiress is to be inspired by the stories of women who have achieved their financial dreams and embody traits such as confidence, persistence, and determination. Some of these women are well-known public figures. Others are women who have achieved amazing success and wealth, but you have probably never heard of them.

They are all women I admire because they believed in themselves and had clear goals. They went after a dream. They were not afraid to make mistakes and learn from them. They realized the faster they failed, the faster they recovered, course-corrected, and succeeded.

Here are brief stories of famous entrepreneurial Wealth Heiresses such as Sara Blakely, J.K. Rowling, Coco Chanel, Oprah Winfrey, Jennifer Lopez, Arianna Huffington, and Debbi Fields, but you don't have to be famous to realize your Wealth Heiress. I chose them to show you they didn't start out with a guarantee of success. I have also included two stories of women you are likely hearing about for the first time: Zhou Qunfei and Judith R. Kaufman. I hope they inspire your Wealth Heiress to see what's possible for you.

Sara Blakely

> *"When I cut the feet out of my pantyhose that one time, I saw it as my sign. I had been visualizing being self-employed prior to this happening. It was my mental preparation meeting the opportunity in that moment."*—Sara Blakely[10]

As the founder of Spanx and the youngest self-made female billionaire in history, Sara came up with the idea of Spanx because she wanted her butt to look better in pants. She sold fax machines door to door, visualized becoming an entrepreneur, and then raised $5,000 to seed her idea. She wrote her own patent and begged manufacturers to make a prototype. They did not understand it and literally thought she was crazy.[11]

After cold-calling buyers, at last she landed a meeting with Neiman Marcus. During the appointment, she sensed the buyer was losing interest. Sara followed her into the ladies' room, modeling the Spanx under her white pants to demonstrate the slimming effect. She got an order for three thousand pairs, and history was made.

Let's review this in slow motion. Sara visualizes being self-employed (her mental image of a finish line). She then gets an idea to fix a problem about the appearance of her derriere and tries to find a solution since she thinks other women may have the same problem. She cuts the feet off a pair of pantyhose to create a prototype (takes action). Reportedly, male manufacturers did not understand her idea, and women needed to be shown the magic of the product.

During her upbringing, her dad taught her to view failure positively. Daily he would ask, "What did you fail at this week?" Sara would tell him, and he would praise her. She learned it was not terrible to fail and that it was good to take risks.[12] She believed in the difference Spanx made on her body and that it would make a difference for other women too. That is what a Wealth Heiress does: She sets her mind, puts a plan into action, and course-corrects until she succeeds.

Sara had no guarantees. She had little money. She did not have manufacturing experience. She saw a problem, created an opportunity to solve it, and believed she could figure it out as she went along. It kept her going through the times her business card was ripped up in front of her or when she was laughed at, but she held the faith that Spanx would work. She did not give up until her goals and her Wealth Heiress were realized, and she course-corrected until she achieved success.

Jennifer Lopez

"Doubt is a killer. You just have to know who you are and what you stand for."

—Jennifer Lopez[13]

How did Jennifer Lopez go from an average working-class family in the Bronx to become a mega celebrity? Jennifer went for her dreams head on. She began her life as a dancer, appearing in stage musicals and music videos. She won a national competition to be on the television show *In Living Color*. Her acting career began with smaller roles and evolved into the lead role in the movie *Selena*. While her dancing, acting, and singing career kept growing, she faced many personal challenges that did not stop her.

Jennifer took risks and ventured from dancing to acting and singing, becoming a major superstar with a net worth estimated at $360 million.[14] She did not stay in her "lane," veering into other mediums.

She had highs and lows, failures and successes. She did not let anyone limit her or tell her she could not act, sing, or be a judge on a talent show. She took chances, tried new things when people warned her not to, and achieved her dreams and her Wealth Heiress, just like you will.

J.K. Rowling

> *"Anything is possible if you've got enough nerve."*
>
> —J.K. Rowling[15]

Author J.K. Rowling grew up in England and always wanted to be a writer. She started writing the first Harry Potter book while she was on welfare. Sometimes, she wrote on old scraps of paper, gradually finishing three chapters, which she submitted to publishers. After a number of rejections, she sold her first book in 1997 for $4,000.

Since then she has sold 450 million copies of Harry Potter, and her movies have grossed $7.7 billion. According to *The Sunday Times* 2017 Rich List, her net worth is about $850 million, not counting the approximately $150 million she has donated to charity. When she was on welfare, do you think she would have believed there was a billionaire Wealth Heiress inside of her? Probably not at first, but she came to believe!

Debbi Fields

> *"You do not have to be superhuman to do what you believe in."*
>
> —Debbi Fields[16]

Have you ever baked chocolate chip cookies? You have, right? It's pretty easy to do if you follow a recipe. In fact, just about anyone can do it. So why did Debbi Fields make millions, and you did not?

Debbi followed her passion, created a vision, and a plan to franchise. She grew up in Oakland, California, with four sisters and loved baking chocolate chip cookies. She founded Mrs. Field's Cookies in

1977, which has grown to over 730 franchised locations in eleven countries. She sold the business in the early 1990s but remains the company's spokesperson.[17]

She had determination, ambition, and courage. She was not a genius. She was not more talented. She thought bigger. She elevated something simple and made a fortune. She set big goals and tapped into the Wealth Heiress that was already within her.

Oprah Winfrey

> *"Create the highest grandest vision possible for your life, because you become what you believe."*

—Oprah[18]

Most of us know Oprah's story, but I believe it is worth repeating. Born into poverty to unmarried parents on an isolated farm in Mississippi, she was raised by her grandparents until she moved to be with her mother and half-brothers in an inner-city Milwaukee neighborhood.

She landed a job in radio while still in high school in Tennessee and began co-anchoring the local evening news at the age of nineteen. Her groundbreaking interview style took a third-rated Chicago talk show to first place. Her success with the *Oprah Winfrey Show* eventually led to the formation of her own production company, HARPO Studio. Today the billionaire runs OWN Productions, an expanding channel that is now in eighty-two million homes.[19]

Let me ask you this: When did Oprah get the ability to create massive wealth? To reach her accomplishments, did she have to do something outside of herself? Or was that ability already inside of her, even when she was poor?

Her Wealth Heiress was there within her all along, waiting to be realized. So is yours. She did not go to a special school to learn how to be "Oprah." She developed her success from deep within, repeating what worked for her and, over time, gaining confidence. Then she spread her wings and took on new challenges and projects.

Judith R. Faulkner

> *"It was painful to be nerdy when I was growing up and I clearly was nerdy. But I think it became a perfectly fine thing to be nerdy after Bill Gates."*

—Judith R. Faulkner[20]

Growing up in New Jersey, Judith enrolled at the University of Wisconsin to pursue a master's degree in computer science. She has since spent her entire adult life in Wisconsin after founding the healthcare records management company Epic in 1979. Eleven years after its founding, she still had only thirty employees. The turning point was when her Windows-based medical-records software stunned the industry and became the industry standard. Today Epic has nine thousand employees, and Faulkner has a net worth of $2.6 billion according to *Forbes*. She is America's wealthiest self-made woman in tech, and she still drives around in a five-year-old Audi.

Judith took the route of higher education and took a risk starting a business. Her success didn't happen overnight but over time with steady improvement. Her Wealth Heiress outsmarted the competition and leapfrogged to the front of the industry. Eventually, her tenacity, intelligence, and ingenuity paid off.

Gabrielle "Coco" Chanel

> *"Success is often achieved by those who don't know that failure is inevitable."*

—Gabrielle "Coco" Chanel[21]

Madame Chanel was raised in an orphanage where she was taught how to sew. She had a brief career as a singer before opening a women's clothing store. As a fashion designer, she was known for elegance, comfort, and simplicity. Her clothes and jewelry were in strong contrast to the opulent and constrictive clothing of the 19th century.

Her firsts were many—launching the first self-named perfume, bringing the "little black dress" to market, and, of course, releasing the classic Chanel suit. She earned the title of "the best designer of her time."[22]

Her life was filled with controversy and legal drama. She was able to overcome attacks to her brand because of her views and understanding of what women wanted. Her immense talent and confidence came from within. Just like Chanel, your Wealth Heiress is within you, ready and able to be realized.

Arianna Huffington

> *"Fearlessness is like a muscle. I know from my own life that the more I exercise it the more natural it becomes to not let my fears run me."*

> —Arianna Huffington[23]

Arianna Stasinopoulos grew up in Greece and studied economics at the University of Cambridge. An author of several books, she married Michael Huffington, a secretary within the U.S. Department of Defense and later a member of the House of Representatives. She ran for governor of California against Arnold Schwarzenegger in 2003 but ended up withdrawing. A pioneer of news media websites, she started *The Huffington Post* in 2005 and then sold it to AOL in 2011 for $315 million. Author of more than a dozen books, today she is an acknowledged international media mogul.[24]

Let's look at Arianna's success. Starting *The Huffington Post* was a stroke of genius and way ahead of her time. She tapped into her Wealth Heiress and developed her abilities. It was always possible. It was always there. Just waiting within her plus, of course, a lot of hard work to make it happen.

Zhou Qunfei

> *"I chose to be in business and I don't regret it."*

> —Zhou Qunfei[25]

Zhou grew up in a small village in central China. Her mother died when she was five, and her father became partially blind in one eye and lost a finger in an industrial accident, so she began raising pigs and ducks to bring in additional food and money for the family. At sixteen, she was forced to drop out of high school and went to work in a watch-lens workshop for one dollar a day. At age twenty-two, she and a few relatives struck out on their own, starting a lens workshop for $3,000.

The business grew steadily, but the turning point was when she decided to make glass screens for mobile phones and touchscreens, including Apple's. Lens Technology now employs over 74,000 people and has thirty-two factories in seven locations. Zhou became the world's richest self-made woman with a net worth of $8 billion.

When Zhou was working for a dollar a day, do you think she knew she would be worth $8 billion one day? Of course not! But through sheer determination, hard work, and course-correcting, she was able to become the world's richest self-made woman. Her Wealth Heiress was within her all along. So is yours.

The Bottom Line

You have untapped potential just waiting for you to take action on your goals. It is up to you to realize the potential within. You can achieve whatever you want. Look at the many examples of women around you, and go for it. And remember that one of the key abilities these women shared is their willingness to take calculated risks. This concept is discussed in the following chapter.

Activate Your Wealth Heiress

1. Take out your Wealth Heiress journal, and write down the names of three people you admire as Wealth Heiresses. Explain what you admire about them and what you believe is their most prominent passions and talent.
2. Create a list of your passions and talents. Examine each and determine how you can parlay them into fulfilling your dreams and making your fortune.

CHAPTER 3

The Nature of Bubbles
and Cycles

*"Everything moves in waves and cycles,
even your investments."*

Two years after my husband died, I was thinking about selling our lovely home in Medina, Washington. The house was too big for just my two beagles and me, and I was pondering when I should sell and where I should move.

I could see the local housing market was booming. One day I counted twenty cranes on the skyline of nearby downtown Bellevue. They were building three thousand high-rise condos, reportedly priced around $1 million each. Rumor was that Bellevue had the second-highest number of cranes in any city, second only to Singapore.

I thought about all the new condos going on the market at the same time. I wondered, "How are they going to sell three thousand million-dollar condos?" It seemed like there would be a lot more supply than demand.

It reminded me of the tech bubble seven years before when stock valuations also seemed to be based on fiction, not facts. People ignored unrealistic valuations, making massive investments right at the peak, probably thinking it would continue a lot longer.

Indeed, there were uncanny similarities between what was happening in the housing market and what had happened at the top of the technology mania. The signs—the similarities to the peak of the tech bubble, the overbuilding of expensive condos, the number of cranes, and homes selling quickly at record prices—were all telling me the boom was about to end.

I decided to put my home up for sale immediately, and it sold in three days at full price with no contingencies, not even a request for an inspection. The fact that it sold so quickly and without even a contingency confirmed my belief that we were near a peak in prices because home inspections and contingencies tend to be waived in strong seller markets.

While waiting for my house to close, newspaper articles about problems with subprime mortgages started appearing, seeming to confirm the real-estate market was beginning to crack and the bubble was close to the end. My house was one of the last to sell at full price. I locked in gains as the bubble was about to peak.

Recognizing the Peak

Bubbles happen when people flock to the same investments, usually because the investments have increased at an accelerated rate for a period of time sufficient for the common observer to think it is a "sure bet." This makes people want to invest.

The reason they are wrong is because they are actually looking in the rearview mirror at *past performance* and thinking that will also be the *future performance*. What they do not realize is that once the trend becomes obvious to everyone, it is about over.

The peak happens when mass psychology takes over and the collective begins to act as one. All at once, people notice the latest bubble is the obvious place to invest, so they buy almost regardless of price. They say, "How have I missed this? This investment has done well. It is the one true investment to hold and never sell. It will continue to increase like it always has."

I heard people say that when large technology companies like Dell, Microsoft, and Intel were peaking in 2000. I heard the same thing when real estate was peaking in 2006 to 2007.

Bubbles are a natural climax to cycles. What I know as an investor is that stocks climb a wall of worry. That means it is normal to be scared you may lose money. However, when you are so sure that your investment cannot lose, that is when you should be worrying. In other words, when you believe real estate cannot lose money or that tech stocks will always go up, this is when you are likely close to the peak of the bubble.

When everyone agrees that a particular investment is going to increase forever, that is when you ought to think about selling. My expression to explain this is that "trees do not grow to the sky." Nothing goes up forever, and investments tend to move in cycles. They have a time they are in favor and a time they are out of favor. You want to own them when they are in favor and sell them at the peak of the bubble while everyone still agrees they will continue to go up in value.

Evidence to Spot Bubbles

How do you recognize bubbles? Certain metrics can be helpful to show you the absurd reality of a bubble's prices. In the case of housing, you can look at price per square foot or how much it will rent for compared to the price. If the annual rent is less than five percent of the market value of the home, be cautious. There's no obvious billboard that says, "This is the peak. Sell." It is much subtler, but it can become glaringly obvious if you know what to look for. That is how I made the decision to sell my home.

Listen to other peoples' conversations, read articles in the newspaper, and pay attention to the covers of magazines. Historically, magazine covers have been indicators either for the peak or the bottom.

The peak often happens when the "everyday person" gets invested. It reminds me of the story of JFK's father, Joe Kennedy, who when given a stock tip by a shoeshine boy sold all his stocks just prior to the stock marketing collapsing in 1929. He reasoned if a shoeshine boy was invested in the stock market, then everyone who could get in was already in, and there was no room for anyone else to get into the market.[26]

I have experienced a similar phenomenon. At the peak of the bubble in technology, cab drivers were giving me unsolicited stock tips. A FedEx deliveryman delivered a package to me and remarked that he was excited that Cisco Systems' stock price had dropped so he could buy some more. I had never met this man before, and he's telling me about his stocks? Those are the kind of crazy things that happen at a peak. You will hear people bragging at cocktail parties about how much money they made in an investment. When that starts happening, it is a sure sign a peak is near.

Another sign of a peak is the television show indicator. I remember there were several television shows showing people how to flip houses. Or obvious schemes like a website where you could flip condos in Florida. Just buy, re-list on the internet, and resell the condo for a profit—without ever setting foot inside. That kind of absurd behavior is typical at the peak of a bubble.

Also toward the peak, people quit their jobs and trade the investment full-time, as if the cycle is so reliable and sustainable they can continue making money at this rate indefinitely. Remember day traders in the tech bubble?

Being able to recognize bubbles will give you a big advantage over most investors. If you understand that bubbles happen at the *end* of a cycle, you can keep an eye out for them, profit from them, and be out before the peak. Since many people do not realize money moves in cycles, they do not realize the cycle will end, and they stay invested too long, causing them financial misfortune.

For example, during the real estate boom from 2000 to 2007, investors who borrowed to buy real estate were handsomely rewarded by rapidly increasing home valuations. However, those who missed the peak of the bubble and stayed leveraged experienced a rapid price decline. Valuations of homes declined below what they paid for them, causing them to lose the houses and the multimillion-dollar fortune they had spent years building.

Lots of investors and homeowners got caught up in the buying frenzy and overpaid. Being able to recognize bubbles helps you see when not to buy, when not to over-leverage, and even when to sell.

A typical business cycle flows like this, clockwise:

Expansion	Boom
Recovery	Recession

When you recognize the flow of expansion, boom, recession, and recovery then you are close to understanding cycles. But that does not explain the ability of some cycle forecasters to be able to predict what would happen on a specific day years in advance.

The Shock of Learning about Cycles

I have been aware of economic cycles such as a pattern of rising and declining inflation since I was young. I remember interest rates were in the double digits and oil was booming. Then interest rates and oil prices started falling, and stocks and bonds did well. Next, real estate boomed. I paid attention to those patterns, but one day in 2007, I heard someone on television who was infinitely more familiar with cycles than I was. His words gave me a whole new perspective—not only on cycles, but also on life.

Dr. Charles Nenner looked more like a mad scientist than a polished Wall Street professional, but he said he was a market timer for Goldman Sachs, so I listened closely. I then researched statements he had made. "Markets do not move at random, and there is no way of influencing their behavior. Markets are part of creation and follow natural laws.... However, once you understand the power of cycles, the correlation to market moves are uncanny. Patterns of past market actions and reactions repeat and are therefore predictable."[27]

Was that true? Could cycles be predictive? Could he know how the stock market would act before everyone else?

He also said: "...do things move at random or don't at random? If they move at random, there's nothing you should read, because you don't know what happens tomorrow. If they don't move at random, then you have to look for the underlying systematic of what happens…. Economic cycles are very long-term cycles, and they are very predictable."[28]

Although I was skeptical, I decided to do some more research to find out if what he was describing was true. This was certainly nothing I had ever heard in the investment industry. Yes, there were waves and patterns that could indicate possible future stock moves, but that was not what he was describing.

I started following Nenner and subscribed to his research. What I learned was that cycles repeat at regular intervals, which make them able to predict future events. I also learned that sometimes—but not always—they are so accurate they can predict an event to the exact day, years in advance.

Cycles can give us a picture of the future and what will happen. Of course, this is a closely guarded secret and something Wall Street vehemently denies. In all of my twenty-five years on Wall Street, I had never heard of anyone able to predict the future with accuracy. Goldman Sachs hired Nenner to create a computer program that incorporated known cycle peaks and troughs.

I talked more with David Gurwitz from Nenner's office. David explained how Nenner was a physician who discovered repeating patterns with stocks. If he could identify a pattern in the past, he could predict that the same thing would happen again. He explained how interest rates moved in thirty-year cycles and real estate moved in eighteen-and-a-half-year cycles. He told me that ahead of us was a stock market crash, a real-estate crash, and a time when the stock market would be closed for a period of time.[29] I was astounded and searched for corroborating evidence.

I found another organization—the Foundation for the Study of Cycles (FSC)—that had been one of the first to discover cycles. I learned that there are 4,200 cycles on the planet that have been documented by FSC, which was started when Herbert Hoover hired Harvard economist Edward Dewey to investigate what caused the Great Depression.[30]

Dewey had been able to eliminate all the reasons you might think caused the depression, such as layoffs and economic policy. Following the 1929 crash and resulting depression, he found that cycles were more useful for predicting economic events than any amount of economic theory that he had learned.[31]

Prominent entrepreneurs like George Westinghouse started backing the research. Other important businessmen in 1931 heard about the project and formed a committee. Out of that committee, the Foundation for the Study of Cycles was born. FSC's founding members included people such as the director of the Bank of England, executives from the Smithsonian, Harvard, Yale, Massachusetts Institute of Technology, Carnegie Institute, Princeton University, McGill University, and representatives from the United Nations. Later, a vice president of the United States and billionaire investors would become prominent members.[32]

The research was astonishing. Economic cycles repeat just like months and seasons do. Edward Dewey stumbled on a series of coincidences that were not only financial, but also extended into weather patterns, migration, animal populations, interest rates, business sales, wars, and plagues. Cycles not only apply to the economy; they exist throughout nature.

The stunning conclusions FSC made are that energy waves impact business, investments, and the financial markets in regularly recurring patterns that make them predictable years in advance. It seemed too fantastic for me to accept until I began to research quantum physics. As quantum physicist Nikola Tesla explains: "If you wish to understand the Universe, think in terms of energy, frequency, and vibration."[33]

I started looking for other people who knew about cycles. In the early 1900s, a cycle researcher named William D. Gann reportedly read cycles and amassed a fortune of $50 million. He made 264 profitable trades out of 286 trades in twenty-five market days.[34] Gann believed in the law of vibration and that stock movements could be determined mathematically using that law:

"Through the law of vibration every stock in the market moves in its own distinctive sphere of activities, as to intensity, volume and direction; all the essential qualities of its evolution are characterized in its own rate of vibration. Stocks, like atoms, are centers of energy;

therefore, they are controlled mathematically. Stocks create their own field of action and power: power to attract and repel, which principle explains why certain stocks at times lead the market and 'turn dead' at other times. Thus, to speculate scientifically it is absolutely necessary to follow natural law."[35]

Lest you think this is foolishness, the New York Stock Exchange apparently does not. A painting of Gann hangs there.

Probably the most proficient cycle researcher is Martin Armstrong. Armstrong was self-taught and stumbled onto cycles by accident when he was a boy. One day he came across a list of financial panics that occurred between 1683 and 1907. He divided the span of 224 years by the number of panics and found out than, on average, there has been a panic every 8.6 years. He discerned a recurrence of major turning points in the economy and in world affairs that followed a distinct and unwavering 8.6-year rhythm. Six cycles of 8.6 years added up to a long-wave cycle of 51.6 years, which separated such phenomena as Black Friday and the commodity panic of 1920, and the Second and Third Punic Wars. My jaw dropped when he said 8.6 years is 3,141 days or pi (3.141) times 1,000. Pi is part of the formula to determine the circumference of a circle—the perfect cycle.[36]

Reportedly, the elite have used knowledge about cycles for generations and kept it among themselves. The Rothschilds, one of the wealthiest families in England, "had broken up the (stock market) price fluctuations into a series of repeating curves that had been combined and used for forecasting."[37] Billionaire stock trader Paul Tudor Jones, who was a board member of FSC, predicted the October 19, 1987, stock market crash and made $100 million in one day by shorting stocks (betting they would go down) when the market declined by twenty-two percent on Black Monday.[38] Just a coincidence or lucky trade? Not when you are talking *that* much money.

How Can You Use Cycles?

I know three things about wealth building. If you understand these things and act on them, you can create tremendous wealth.

- Money moves in cycles.

- Cycles peak in bubbles.
- To be savvy with money you need to be aware of bubbles and cycles.

It is powerful to consider bubbles and cycles in your wealth building because it may help you identify when a bubble exists. You might want to take more risk or be aware that there are times when investments get ahead of themselves and that is not the time to jump in. To build wealth, you must compound your money at a high rate and understand that bubbles and cycles are real, which will help prevent you from making mistakes.

For example, I know we are close to the top if the most inexperienced investor is touted as the new "expert" investor, if predicting the stock market will continue to rise forever with very aggressive forecasts, or if people are checking their 401(k) accounts daily. If bad news disappears from financial channels, that is another sign. If billionaires are selling stock in a publicly traded company (which they usually do ahead of the crowd because they have access to cycle research), I pay attention. I watch what they *do*, not what they say.

If interest rates are rising and the Federal Reserve Board is taking money out of the market, this tells me the economy is being encouraged to contract. When the Federal Reserve Board prints money and floods the system with liquidity, the opposite is true, and money will find its way into investments like stocks and real estate. Watch for whatever is at an all-time peak. That is a clue it is about to reverse.

When master investor Bernard Baruch was asked how he made so much money in the stock market, he replied, "I made my money by selling too soon."[39] If you wait until the reason to sell is obvious, you are likely not going to get out ahead of anyone else. Markets decline when there are mostly sellers but no buyers. It is like hitting an air pocket, and markets can decline quickly, causing panics. They happen regularly. Every ten years or so, we experience a 20 percent decline in the stock market. Rather than denying it, we should embrace the ability to buy low once every ten years when stocks are "on sale."

I am not suggesting you try to time the market. Rather, I am suggesting there are times when bubbles become obvious, but people either do not see it or take any action. If you had some cash on hand to buy when the market went down, you would be buying when risk was less and at a bargain price.

Investing in trends provides a tremendous way to build wealth. The media likes to portray bubbles as a negative thing, and they certainly are when they peak and pop. But prior to that pinnacle event, they provide the greatest potential to create a fortune. It is important to realize that bubbles start out as undervalued assets that have been out of favor for a long time. Then gradually, they become the hot place to invest as the cycle peaks in a bubble.

The Bottom Line

Money moves in cycles and peaks in bubbles. They happen regularly. Rather than fear them, they should be anticipated and embraced so you can buy low and sell high. To do this, you need to be aware of the exuberance or fear around you and discern for yourself when a peak has topped or bottomed out.

Activate Your Wealth Heiress

1. Write in your Wealth Heiress journal the conversations you are hearing through your neighbors, your friends, and social media. Is everyone talking about how much money they've made in their 401(k)s? Are they bragging about how much money they have made in real estate? Are they touting a particular stock? These may be signs if they are in the extreme. Write down what you are seeing and hearing in your journal.
2. If an investment is popular with everyone you know, it may indicate the end of the cycle is near. What trends do you notice a lot of friends and relatives investing in? Make observations. Are interest rates moving higher or lower? If interest rates are in a rising cycle, could that mean real-estate prices will slow or even fall? Understand trends help you navigate the economy, cycles, and investments.

CHAPTER 4

Why Calculated Risk
Is a Good Thing

*"To manifest wealth you must let go
of fear and take some risk."*

When talking about risk, it is easy to visualize a gambling casino in which dice are thrown and the outcome seems completely random. That is not the risk I am talking about. The risk I am talking about is calculated and not a matter of luck.

Women can learn to take calculated risk by diversifying and being successful investors. Studies show women actually have better investing records than men do.[40] Over time, women have a slightly better investment record than men, mainly because women hold onto the stock longer while men give up sooner on an investment that's not performing and move on to another.

Calculated risk comes into play in wealth building in compounding—the magic that Einstein called the "eighth wonder of the world."[41] Compounding is something we learn about when we're about ten years old in school, and it is an important wealth-building concept. It is the "c" in my Wealth Building Formula, which will be discussed later in this book. So how are risk and compounding related?

Calculated Risk Yields Higher Returns

Taking some risk is an important part of wealth building because it is what allows you to receive higher returns, and higher returns lead to more wealth. Let's compare Sara and Jessica.

Sara is not comfortable with risk, so she leaves $50,000 she inherited in her bank account, currently earning one percent interest.

Jessica is comfortable with some risk-taking and knows that she must choose an investment with more risk than a bank account in order to grow her money. She invests in a mutual fund, which provides diversification and professional management. By investing in the stock market, over time Jessica is potentially increasing her rate of return from one percent to ten percent.

When comparing the difference in that one decision over fifteen years, Sara's bank account would be worth $8,000 more or $58,048, while Jessica's mutual fund would be worth $208,862, or $150,814 more than Sara's. Taking more risk paid off for Jessica.

If you have a long term time horizon and more to invest, taking some risk in the stock market may allow you to average close to a ten percent return over thirty years in your retirement account. Compare the difference if you were starting with $200,000 in your retirement account. Taking no risk and earning one percent, you would end up with $269,569 versus having $3,489,880 by taking a calculated risk. That is a difference of over $3,200,000.

If you are content to leave your money in a savings account at one percent interest, it will take you seventy-two years to double your money. You are not going to reach your retirement goals that way. You have got to invest in something that will give you the potential for a higher return.

Calculated risk means you know the potential risks involved, but it is worth doing anyway because the rewards are so great. You are not gambling. You are not leaving things to chance. You are putting the odds in your favor because that is what the stock market with an eighty-year long-term track record of about ten percent teaches you. Is it possible that track record would not repeat itself? Yes, it is possible, but considering the additional profit potential, I think you have to agree it is worth the risk.

Calculated Risk and the Stock Market

Many women become good judges of stocks because they make shopping decisions every day. You know what you want to buy and what you do not. You know the popular brands. You know what's good quality whether it is a shoe, car, or restaurant.

Stocks are merely brands—companies that have offered some of their shares to the public. When you invest in a share of stock in Michael Kors, you are a co-owner of the company with the founder. Companies like Michael Kors sell stock to raise money to be able to develop new products, reach more customers, and make more money.

Let's say, for example, Tory Burch wanted to open some more boutiques because presumably opening more boutiques globally will sell more goods and make more money. She wants to raise money to open fifty additional boutiques and expand the brand, so she decides to give up her private investor status and become a public owner.

Instead of keeping her financial records to herself and confidential, she allows potential investors to see her company financials to decide if they want to own a piece of her company. She hires an investment banker to create and offer shares in her company to the public in an initial public offering (IPO).

If 1,000,000 shares are issued at $10 a share, she will raise $10 million. Of course, she keeps some of the stock for herself to maintain ownership and possibly majority control, but she can use the capital to open more boutiques. If her profits increase, the value of her shares will increase. Shareholders win, and she wins.

Stocks are just companies with brands, and many stocks that perform well are likely some of your favorite brands. They encompass the cars you drive, beverages you drink, computers you use, stores where you shop, social media you interact with, travel agencies, plane manufacturers, gasoline companies, food, work-out clothing, make-up stores, and everything that makes you a happy consumer.

The stocks of many of your favorites may have been very successful investments. They are simply brands to which consumers are very loyal and which continue to gain market share and profits.

Financial advisors always remind us that past performance is no guarantee of future results, but you have to take investing in the stock market into account because of its long-term track record. Most of the time what is driving the stock market are earnings of companies. Are companies growing and earning more? Are they getting more sales and customers? Are they introducing new products and services?

Calculated Risk and Bonds

Bonds are IOUs where someone borrows money and pays it back with interest. If the government borrows money, it is a Treasury note or bond. If a company borrows money, it is a corporate bond. If the company does not have strong financials, they have to pay more interest to borrow. That is called a junk bond because of the risk that the company could default and not pay the money back, thereby making it like "junk." Years ago, many casinos in Las Vegas were financed with junk bonds. They paid investors high interest rates so they could borrow money and build the casinos.

Smart Diversification

Diversification is part of investing in your 401(k). You are making decisions about your asset allocation so that you own a collection of different investments. You want to make sure you have some money in large companies (large caps), medium companies (mid-caps), small companies (small caps), international (large companies outside of the U.S., mostly in Europe), and emerging markets (companies in up-and-coming economies such as Brazil, Russia, India, China, and South Africa, which are often called the BRICS). By spreading your money around, you are taking advantage of more growth areas available to you.

To Hold or Not to Hold

Buying and holding investments for the long term is a good strategy that has worked for many investors. The big money is made over years of holding onto companies, one of the reasons investing icon Warren Buffett says, "When we own portions of outstanding businesses with outstanding managements, our favorite holding period is forever."[42]

There are times that markets can get ahead of themselves and become overvalued. Sharp pullbacks are inevitable, which I will talk about later. I have seen that happen many times in my lifetime. Usually in a ten-year period, though, stock performance will average out and get back to positive returns.

Still, when you see a market that is obviously overvalued, like in 2000 with stocks or in 2007 with real estate, it does not hurt to take some money off the table and give yourself some cash to take advantage of bargains. The only problem is it can be scary to invest when the world seems to be coming to an end, so you really have to be what's known as a "contrarian" investor.

Being a contrarian means you are going in the opposite direction from the crowd. When they are super optimistic, you are cautious. When they are selling, you are buying. When they are pessimistic, you see opportunity. You have to go the opposite of what the pundits are saying on television. They will be most pessimistic at the bottom and most optimistic at the peak.

Take Advantage of Fluctuations

Taking calculated risks means you are subjecting your investments to fluctuations that can be temporarily uncomfortable. Fluctuation means prices are going to move up and down. It can feel like a roller coaster and be emotionally hard to take.

You have to think about investments the way you think about shopping at a high-end retailer. Many luxury goods sell for a premium price, but once in a while, they go on sale. When they do, you snatch them up. Stocks are the same way.

Stocks come arranged in nice packages called mutual funds or exchange-traded funds (ETFs). A mutual fund is a group of stocks selected by a designated professional portfolio manager who is incentivized to get a higher return than the average performance for the stock market. He or she will pick the stocks they like and put them in an equity (stock) mutual fund and decide when to buy and sell stocks. The average they are measured against is typically the Standard & Poor's 500, the five hundred largest companies in the United States. It includes many household names like Exxon, McDonald's, Apple, Microsoft, Amazon, Facebook, Johnson & Johnson, Google, Chevron, Bank of America, The Home Depot, and more.

The S&P 500 is an index fund that tracks the stock market. Gains or losses in the market are measured by indexes like this. When we say the stock market averages 10 percent per year, it means the S&P 500 has averaged approximately 10 percent over the long term.

Portfolio managers are paid to try to beat the performance of the S&P 500. If they do, they get paid more and you earn more, so it is a win–win. The only problem is that most managers have a hard time beating the averages so the trend is just to buy the average or the S&P 500.

Exchange Traded Funds (ETFs) invest in indexes like the S&P 500. Because there is no portfolio manager managing the fund, it merely mirrors the S&P 500. It is known as a passive managed fund because the stocks do not change. ETFs have gained popularity because many portfolio managers have not outperformed the S&P 500, so why pay them an additional fee when you are not earning more? Conventional wisdom says put your money in indexes that are lower cost and mirror the stock market's performance.

There are quality companies, ETFs, or mutual funds you want to own. When they go on sale, you want to buy more. Instead, most investors get scared and sell at exactly the wrong time. Usually investments will bounce up sharply after a decline, so selling prevents you from gaining back some of the loss from the big bounce. The time to sell is not after a big decline, but when there is wild optimism in anticipation of more gains.

When sentiment surveys show that optimistic investors believe the stock market will go up (known as "bullish"), you can almost guarantee there will be some kind of a decline coming. That is the time to take a little money off the table, not when the market drops. When it drops, you want to have cash to buy on sale.

That is where the concept of dollar cost averaging (DCA) comes in. When you DCA, it just means you are having money automatically come out of your account and into an investment. For example, you allocate $200 monthly from your bank account to invest into an index fund. Shares are purchased at whatever the current price is. Since the price of the fund fluctuates each month, sometimes you are paying more and sometimes you are paying less for the shares.

Just like in your 401(k), the purchases are made for the same dollar amount every month. If the price has dropped on a fund, you will buy more shares. If the price has gone up, you will buy fewer shares. Over time, studies have shown that your average cost will be lower than if you invested the same amount all at once.[43] Buying in a systematized, automated way helps to take the emotion out and is a very smart way to invest.

Go Beyond Your 401(k)

I started dollar-cost averaging in my 20s, and it taught me about investing, fluctuation, and staying in for the long term. The sooner you start, the better off you will be.

Even if you are investing monthly in a 401(k) plan at work, I still recommend that you also invest outside of your 401(k) into the stock market. Even $100 a month will be $1200 annually and will add up over time in your investments. Shoot for saving 20 percent of your income each month. If you cannot save that much at first, try to work up to it.

Mutual fund companies are happy to DCA for you and usually do not charge to do it. Of course, you will pay a commission to buy the mutual fund or ETF, but that is a small price to pay and will help you compound your money over time. You can usually get started for as little as $100 a month, so just about anyone can do it. One brokerage even waives their minimum $1,000 to open an account if you have $100 automatic monthly transfers.

Once in a while, I run across women who think investing in stocks is like gambling. I disagree. Gambling is based on mostly luck—getting good cards. Investing is definitely not luck; it requires skill and knowledge.

Think of it this way: When you go shopping, you know the brands you want to buy. You know which brands you are loyal to. Why is that? One of the reasons is they have proven themselves with quality and consistency. You like the yoga or athletic wear at a particular store, so you go back over and over again. Investing is like that. Some of the companies on the stock exchange are simply brands that consumers buy over and over. They continue to gain market share and have more and more success. As they grow, the value of their shares grows, which is how as an investor you make more money.

But stock picking is not about just buying your favorite brands, because it is about the consistency of the earnings/profits of the company. A retailer might be hot for a while with teenagers and sell out their merchandise, only to turn cold later. The stock price will likely reflect that fickleness and will go down.

Also, profit margins have to be considered. Cars, for example, are very expensive to manufacture. A technology company like Google, however, does not have to manufacture anything so its profit margins would naturally be higher. High profit margins make companies very attractive to investors since so much money goes right to the bottom line. Pay attention to your favorite tech companies and think about their profit margins. Are they a mostly virtual company like Google, or do they have to pay for employees, plants, raw materials and equipment? Thinking about the business model of the company can help determine if you want to invest in it. Of course, some companies with high expenses like defense contractors and airline manufacturers can still make a lot of money.

Once a company is on your radar screen, check out the consistency of its profitability. Are they profitable one quarter and not the next? That is not good. You want a company that is growing consistently and may be even growing at a faster rate each quarter.

In this age of technology, rules are changing. New companies are emerging that did not exist in the past, and they are extremely profitable. Google stock has averaged 26 percent per year since its 2004 initial public offering (IPO).[44] That means $10,000 invested in Google (Alphabet) would have grown to $201,751 in fourteen years. The next Google is still out there for you to discover and invest in.

Investing is definitely not gambling. In fact, if you are doing it right, you are taking into account a lot of information that takes the risk out of the investment. By buying stocks that are consistent with earnings, good quality, and growing, you are choosing the cream of the crop. Just like popular brands, the best quality stocks are always in demand and will be widely owned.

The speculative ones are the investments that are low priced (often "penny stocks," which by definition sell under $5 a share). You want to stay away from these and any get-rich-quick stocks touted on blogs or in emails. Stick with quality and brands you know are consistently growing, not the flash in the pan.

Embrace Volatility

You cannot control the stock market, so try not to beat yourself up when the big declines do happen. About every ten years, it is normal for the market to drop 20 percent, so expect it.

Rather than fear volatility, embrace it. The market will usually bounce back over time, so the best thing to do is often nothing. If you have not freed up cash to go bargain hunting after a 20 percent drop, it is too late to sell. So the best thing to do is nothing. Just know big drops in the stock market from time to time will happen. Anticipate them and do not fight them. Be prepared by taking a little money off the table when consumer sentiment peaks so you have some cash to buy bargains. This line of thinking will serve you well.

If you do not want to take the time to do this, it is perfectly fine too. It is not necessary at all. You can simply buy and hold. Just keep a level head during the big declines and know that the worst thing you can do is panic and sell when stocks have fallen. The best thing to do is absolutely nothing.

Roth and Traditional IRAs

IRAs are great savings vehicles because they allow you to have tax advantages with your retirement savings. There are traditional IRAs and Roth IRAs. Currently, you can contribute $5,500 to a Roth or traditional IRA and people over age fifty can contribute an additional $1,000 for a total of $6,500. You pay income taxes upfront on a Roth IRA. After that, all growth and withdrawals are tax-free. A Roth IRA has better tax advantages.

The problem is people who earn over a certain amount cannot contribute to a Roth. For single filers in 2018, that income threshold starts at $120,000 and caps at $135,000. In that range, your contribution is limited, eventually reaching zero. For married filing-jointly filers and qualifying widows/widowers in 2018, that income threshold starts at $189,000 and caps at $199,000.[45]

If your income exceeds the Roth IRA limits, you can still invest money into a traditional IRA and then convert it to a Roth. There are no income limits for doing that.

Unlike traditional IRAs, which require you to start taking withdrawals at age 70 ½, a Roth IRA can accumulate for your entire life. If you contribute $5,000 to a Roth IRA every year for forty years and earn 10 percent, you will end up with $2,660,555, all of which can be withdrawn completely tax-free. You must have a Roth account for at least five years before you can withdraw money. There is still a 10 percent early withdrawal penalty for taking money out before you are age 59 ½. Please talk to your tax preparer for details for your particular situation.

The Bottom Line

In order to achieve your goal of financial freedom, you have to compound at the highest rate you can while taking a moderate amount of risk. That means it is most likely in your best interest to invest in the stock market as soon as possible.

By investing in stocks, you are able to compound at a higher rate, historically an average of about 10 percent. Investing will build wealth for you much faster and allow you to have more money than if you do not own stocks/ETFs/mutual funds. The first and best place to start is usually your 401(k) plan at work, if you have one, or an IRA if you do not.

Activate Your Wealth Heiress

1. Take a look at your 401(k) and at a minimum consider diversifying into a large cap, mid cap, small cap and international fund. If you do not have a 401(k), start a Roth or traditional IRA, depending on what you qualify for with a brokerage firm and invest in low-fee mutual funds or ETFs.

CHAPTER 5

The Six Steps to Wealth

*"The Six Steps to Wealth is my step-by-step
system of how to become wealthy."*

Wealth was something that was all around me growing up. Some of
the kids I went to school with had sprawling lakefront homes with
panoramic city skyline views, yachts, fancy cars, and designer clothes.
I did not have those things. I began to wonder—why are some people rich? What did they do to become rich? Was it learnable? If I
could figure out how they did it, maybe I could become rich too.

After high school, I went to the University of Washington and
got a B.A. in Business. I was eager to go to work, earn a paycheck,
and get started with my wealth building. I got a job with a local stock
brokerage firm in Seattle in the financial planning department. For
the next twenty-five years, I worked in various capacities of support,
sales, and management in the financial industry.

My starting salary was a paltry $9,000 a year, but within five
years, I was earning $100,000 in salary and commissions, market-
ing investments to my clients—financial advisors. Over the years,
I marketed investments such as mutual funds, insurance, separately
managed accounts, and hedge funds.

I loved learning about investing and working with portfolio managers who shared their investment strategies with me. My job was to

know everything about how portfolio managers were investing the money, their strategies, and long-term track records. My work took me from Seattle to New York. Many years later, on 9/11/01, when I saw the planes hit the World Trade Center, I prayed for my managers and colleagues who were attending a meeting in the building. My co-workers narrowly escaped the collapsing buildings although, sadly, we lost one of our colleagues that day.

My job in the financial industry centered around portfolio managers managing clients' money, so the message was drilled into us and we, in turn, drilled it into the public that you should not manage money yourself. The message was clear: Do not try this at home. Investing in individual stocks was discouraged because it was seen as too risky.

The industry taught me that you should buy mutual funds and hold them forever. Yet I rarely met anyone who became wealthy by owning mutual funds, and I never knew anyone under age sixty-five who did. I really did not want to wait until I was in my sixties to enjoy life and have enough money to live my dreams. I started looking at where I could invest and compound money.

I invested in real estate, buying a couple of condos for myself, and I had some success. Later I met a realtor who introduced me to a financial partner, and we invested and rehabbed luxury homes. I handled the projects, and he supplied excess capital beyond what I could afford. Although our flips produced about a 15-percent return, the process of fixing up a house and selling it was a lot of work, and it was not enjoyable. I still had a grueling full-time job, traveling four days a week, and was managing these projects on the side.

I noticed the stock market had gained close to 30 percent one year. Stocks seemed like a lot less work than rehabbing houses. Because of my understanding of the power of compounding based on my observations of millionaires, it made me think this could be more profitable.

I picked up *How to Make Money in Stocks* by William J. O'Neil and read everything I could about how to buy stocks. It was the turning point. My realization that stocks were the favored cycle combined with my knowledge of how to buy stocks set me up to be in the right place and the right time. The result was the creation of a $2 million fortune that surprised even me.

My Investing Success

I am the first to admit I got lucky. There was no way to know that when I made my foray into individual stocks that the all-time greatest shift in technology was about to come along—the internet. In those days, which seem like ancient times now, not many people understood what the internet was. Even Bill Gates, the founder of Microsoft, did not understand it and was late to invest because he did not see the internet's importance.

Neither did I, of course. Someone once said that success is where luck and preparation meet, and that is exactly where I was. In the middle of it all. Very lucky. I did have some theories, though.

One was that the demographics of baby boomers coming into their peak years earning and investing for retirement were causing the stock market to go up.[46] Harry Dent's book, *The Great Boom Ahead,* had a big impact on me and helped me hold on through horrific volatility that would cause my portfolio to go down 40 percent or more. I'd get bummed out and kick myself, but I hung on. Eventually the market always seemed to turn around and start going up again, erasing my losses and moving to new highs.

My other theorem was that new technology was being purchased by corporate America as we were getting close to the calendar year turning 2000, known as Y2K. I knew firsthand that banks had opened their budgets and were spending whatever it took to be ready for the millennium. I had worked a year at a regional bank after marrying Roger so I could be at home more. All banks had to comply with regulations and overcome the potential software glitch built into their software that might cause the date to roll back to 1900 instead of 2000.

Y2K was terrifying businesses, so everyone was upgrading to new software and hardware, fueling a tech boom. At the same time, the internet was being introduced and dot-coms were launching with easy money from investors. It was called the New Economy, and everyone was getting rich.

I think it is easier to risk more when you do not have that much; risk becomes harder the more you have. Today I am a lot more conservative and cautious, but back then I'd get up early at 4 or 5 a.m., study stocks, and pick my trades. I had to clear them with my compliance department first because they did not want anyone in my department buying the same stocks on the same day as the portfolio managers. They were three hours ahead, so I'd fax in my paperwork and get back an approval before making a trade.

I was comfortable investing in the leading tech companies like Microsoft, Dell, Cisco Systems, Intel, AOL, eBay, Amazon, and Nokia, among others. They had excellent profits and were "real" companies versus some of the high fliers that had no earnings but were all fluff. Companies like Pets.com and Webvan were new concepts that had strong debuts, but thankfully I avoided the "revenues do not matter anymore, only the number of eyeballs and clicks matter" mindset.

My husband was skeptical but started to become a believer as our portfolio grew. It started growing so fast I began to keep track of the balance every day and reported it to him. There were a couple of heady days in 1999 when it grew $100,000 in one day. I had failures too. I took a risk and bought options on Amazon, thinking it was going to go up a lot. I was right about that but wrong on the timing, which meant I lost the whole $13,000 I invested. No more options trading for me.

My best trade was getting out of Microsoft near its all-time high. The open source operating system LINUX gained popularity, and I was worried it could hurt Microsoft or at least its earnings. I sold our whole position, and it would be another seventeen years before Microsoft's price would surpass what I sold it for.

At the end of 1999, the calendar year turned over to 2000 without a glitch, but stocks were getting out of control. Our joint accounts crossed $2 million, and a million of that was made in one year alone. People started quitting their jobs to day trade stocks. Headlines on magazine covers asked, "Are you rich yet?" Everyone seemed to be getting rich. At work, we launched a Tech Fund, mirroring an institutional fund that finished 1999 up 100 percent. Everyone wanted to participate in it, and the fund raised a billion dollars.

On March 10, 2000, the bull market ended and turned into a vicious bear, heading down for the next two years before bottoming. I recognized the signs of a bubble, but it went on for months beyond what I expected. Everyone believed the mantra "buy the dips," so how were they to know everything had changed?

Fortunately, one of my theories—that much of the tech boom was due to Y2K spending—helped me see why profits were slowing down. It was as if corporations just stopped purchasing hardware and software, and some of the prior leaders seemed to be in a free fall. I could understand why, but it surprised the crowds to see profits quickly falling off a cliff.

I did the best I could. The volatility was crazy, and I certainly did not do everything perfectly. We lost some money getting out of over-valued stocks. But investing is about the long term, and over time our net worth continued to grow. I felt a real sense of accomplishment. My experiences clarified what it took to build wealth. I put that knowledge into a clear explanation called the Six Steps to Wealth, and I am sharing them with you. First, I'll give you a short introduction of each step so you get a sense of the flow. There is a full chapter on each one.

Step One: Create a Wealthy Mindset

I believe a wealthy mindset is the foundation of all wealth. One of the best books that I think was ever written about wealth is *Think and Grow Rich* by Napoleon Hill, who interviewed the wealthiest men of his time and documented their methods.

Hill had special access because Andrew Carnegie, one of the richest men and whose foundation we can thank for building 2,509 libraries worldwide, arranged interviews with the five hundred wealthiest men in the 1930s. Carnegie wanted to have Hill share knowledge in a book compiled from the interviews.

That book was the source of the phrase "thoughts are things." It connected mindset and wealth building. So when I tell you step one is to create a wealthy mindset, it is not without substantiation. Another phrase that came from that book is, "Whatever the mind of man can conceive and believe it can achieve."[47]

I like to say it a little differently: "Whatever you can believe with *certainty* you will accomplish, you will." The problem is our brain is swimming in negative thoughts, so it is difficult to think positively, let alone with certainty. On average, our brains think 98 percent of the same things we thought yesterday, and 80 percent of those thoughts are negative.[48]

Our beliefs are influenced by ideas from our family, experiences, and culture that we learn at a young age. Our subconscious mind holds beliefs about money that we may not even be aware of consciously, so we often have a hidden inner battle going on. That makes it hard to believe we can do it.

Reprogramming your subconscious mind is critical to making changes that will be reflected on a conscious level. I recommend you use affirmations and repetition to make the changes in your subconscious belief system. More on that later.

Let setting a goal and focusing on it propel you to take action toward achieving it. If you are starting a journey, you need to move in that direction and take a first step to get going. You can always correct your path later if you get off course. It is important just to get started. More detail on this step can be found in chapter 6.

Step Two: Save a Nest Egg

We've been told it is not possible for the average person to become a millionaire; it requires dishonesty; money is evil; and if we are frugal enough, we can become wealthy. We've been told if we pay off all debt, do not spend, work harder, and get a great FICO score, then all will be well.

Bullpuckey.

We've focused on the minutia for so long that people think *not* spending three dollars on a latte is the answer to financial success. Or that couponing is where to focus all our time. Or budgets are the Holy Grail. Certainly, these things can save money, but they will not make you rich. Nope. Instead of the small stuff, we need to focus on the *big* stuff.

Please understand: Saving three dollars a day by not buying lattes is a step in the right direction, but it may not be enough. Understanding how your behavior handling your largest expenses like homes and cars keeps you from reaching your retirement goals will make a bigger difference than forgoing lattes.

Let's talk about buying homes, one of the largest purchases we make in our lifetimes. There's a common view that it is perfectly fine to buy and sell homes and move often. It is just not smart. You can spend tens and even hundreds of thousands of dollars in moving costs, real estate commissions, mortgage points, home repairs, and remodeling if you are constantly moving on up.

Look at this example: Susan and Tom want to buy a new home. They lived in the home they were in for three years but decided they did not like the neighborhood. They bought a condo in an urban neighborhood but then decided they wanted a house instead of a condo, so they moved a third time.

Let's say each home cost the same $500,000 with closing costs at 2 to 5 percent. Multiplying closing costs by three moves is 6 percent (three times 2 percent) to 15 percent (three times 5 percent) of $500,000. They have now spent from $30,000 to $75,000. Then there are costs to fix up their house for sale plus remodeling the new home they buy. That could run $2,000 to $50,000 or more for each house, multiplied by three is $6,000 to $150,000. Add real-estate commissions of 6 percent to two of the moves or $60,000. In total, Susan and Tom have spent $96,000 to $360,000.

If instead of paying those costs they had invested it at 10 percent for thirty years, they could have made $1.7 to $6.3 million. Do you see how it is big mistakes like moving frequently that can keep you from attaining wealth?

What I recommend is being very clear where and why you are buying a home so you do not have to move for twenty years or even longer. If you just got married and know you are going to have children, buy your home in a good school district. Buying once and living there as long as you can is your best strategy for wealth building. Now you see why.

Of course, circumstances can change and cause you to need to move. My point is if moving is completely elective and not for a very good reason, do not do it. Stay where you are and use the money you saved to remodel your home.

Besides being smart about your largest purchases, you also need to accumulate some money to start investing. There are many ways to do this, and I am sure you can be creative and decide how to build a nest egg account by saving, selling, sharing, or servicing. You can save money by spending less and saving the difference, selling things you own or purchase online, sharing and pooling money with other investors, or performing a service for others on the side to collect extra money. We will talk more about how to accumulate money in chapter 7.

Step Three: Find a Mentor and Become Knowledgeable

You need someone to teach you the ropes. A mentor has done something you want to accomplish and can shorten the path for you. Make sure your mentors for becoming a millionaire (but not necessarily your financial advisors) have achieved wealth for themselves.

A mentor provides knowledge for you. He or she teaches you things that cannot typically be learned from logic. For example, many financial experts say to become wealthy, all you have to do is spend less than you earn. That is not true unless you make a very high income, but for most people, it is not the way it works because you need to invest and compound too.

In reality, it is *all about* the investing and compounding. If you do not compound at high enough rates, you would not build wealth in your lifetime. For example, if your money is earning 2 percent in a savings account, it will take thirty-six years for the money to double, but if you can earn 10 percent, your money will double in 7.2 years. It is called the "Rule of 72."

In the Rule of 72, the number of years times the interest rate always equals seventy-two. So money would double at 8 percent for nine years ($8 \times 9 = 72$) and at 9 percent for eight years. It would double at 6 percent in twelve years and at 12 percent in six years. They all equal seventy-two. Just know this: *The higher the rate you compound money, the sooner you will have financial freedom.*

Follow someone who has accomplished what you want to accomplish, so they can show you the direct route. The important thing is that they have done it. You will learn more about finding a mentor and becoming knowledgeable in chapter 10.

Step Four: Invest in a Money Engine

A money engine is simply something that grows your wealth. We've already explored some of those in the chapter about taking calculated risks. An investment is simply the money engine that will take you to your destination.

There are many different types of vehicles that have engines, and there is no *one* way. If you want to get from Los Angeles to New

York City, you can ride a motorcycle, car, train, bus, or plane. The speed with which you will arrive depends on the vehicle you choose and how fast it is traveling or, in this case, growing. Investments are the same way. You can invest in stocks, mutual funds, ETFs, or real estate. One way might be faster than another in terms of compounding rate depending on the cycle and other factors.

Look forward to determine where to invest. Do not just look in the rear-view mirror. Most investors are trained to look at performance from the prior decade. That has nothing to do with the next decade. In fact, it is likely that the next decade's best performance will not come from the same place it did during the previous decade because it is already high.

For example, the bond market had a spectacular thirty-year cycle. Interest rates peaked in 1980 at a 20 percent Fed Funds rate, which is the cost financial institutions charge each other for money. Once interest rates started coming down, bond interest rates also dropped. As interest rates decline, the value of a bond rises, so dropping interest rates provide gains on bonds.

What happens when the opposite occurs? When interest rates rise? Bond valuations decline. So if you expected bonds to go up after interest rates started to rise, you would be mistaken. The value of a bond will not move the same way in a rising interest rate market as it did in a falling interest rate market, yet asset allocation models still suggest large percentages of long term bonds in your portfolio as if they are "safe." They aren't always safe in a rising-interest-rate environment. It is impossible for bonds to have the gains they had in the last cycle when rates are rising from 2 percent today.

Look instead for what the next business cycle, interest rate cycle, and inflation cycle will likely bring. If we are at near-zero interest rates, they can only go one direction in the future. If we are at low inflation, it is likely to go up. If we are in a recession, eventually it will recover. If the economy is booming, the next phase is likely a recession.

Stocks and commodities often trade in twenty- to thirty-year cycles. From 1966 to 1982, commodities outperformed stocks. From 1982 to 2007, stocks outperformed everything else. Usually the last bubble is not the next bubble again for a long, long time.

Historically, most millionaires made their first million in their own business or in real estate, but also in stocks, stock options, oil, and commodities. It depended on the timing of the trend. To build wealth quickly, the investment you choose should create a high return on investment (ROI). That rate times your nest egg compounded is the engine that will propel you to wealth.

There's no one right road, just like there's no one type of transportation. Some transportation is faster than others, and that's the same as your investment engine. You will learn more about this in chapter 11.

Step Five: Compound at a High Rate

The higher the rate you can compound your money, the faster you will grow your wealth. Focusing on the compounding rate was the key to achieving my goals sooner. Again, this was the breakthrough insight for me. Compounding means your money earns interest, and the money you earn on your interest earns interest.

Compounding starts out slowly and then increases exponentially. The more time you have or the higher the rate at which you can compound money consistently, the faster you will build wealth. For example, if you invested $10,000 annually compounding at 100 percent, your investment will grow to one million dollars in about seven years.

Is 100 percent compounding an unreasonable rate to expect? Yes, in most cases. However, if you are using other people's money or leveraging to build wealth, it raises your rate of return dramatically. Also, small businesses can realistically grow at 100 percent at least for the first several years. That is why real estate and small business owners are the most common millionaires.

Compounding is the most crucial step of the Six Steps to Wealth. It is important to earn the highest rate you can and *not to withdraw any funds from the investment.* If you make the mistake of withdrawing money from the account in the early years, it will set your wealth building back. For example, if you invested $100,000 for thirty years at 10 percent, you would have $1,744,940, but if you withdrew $20,000 in year five, you would only have $1,027,827. In other words, the $20,000 withdrawal really cost you $717,113.

Wealthy people understand compounding well. For example, Teresa worked for an insurance company owned by a billionaire. She said the owner was laser-focused on his company earning 10 percent every year. He shared his goal with the entire company, and everyone's bonus depended on achieving the magic 10 percent. Now maybe it makes sense to you that his knowledge and focus on compounding is probably what made him a billionaire. It's important for your Wealth Heiress to grasp the importance of compounding. You will learn more about the ins and outs of compounding in chapter 12.

Step Six: Protect Your Wealth

It's important to retain the wealth you created and not lose it. A wealth builder can leverage to build their wealth, but once it is built, they need to eliminate the leverage to keep and protect their wealth.

Once you have achieved wealth, it is important to pay off your debt and then diversify. If you do not, and remain leveraged, that leverage can sink your net worth as fast as it built it if the asset depreciates or the market declines.

Taylor was borrowing money to buy real estate in Scottsdale. As soon as properties increased in value, they were used as collateral to buy more properties. Since home values kept rising, this cycle was repeated over and over. Unfortunately, instead of being satisfied with creating millions and stopping at a reasonable point, Taylor kept leveraging and never paid off the original debt, only to lose it all when the housing market crashed.

I have seen a lot of money made by leveraging and buying a strong performing investment engine, only to be lost when that investment trend stops. Diversifying can help protect your wealth. It is a defensive measure, not an offensive measure. Millionaires know it slows your wealth building on the way up, but it also protects you from ruin in a declining market.

You also need to protect your wealth legally with wills and against the unexpected with insurance. We will talk more about that in chapter 13.

What Oscar de la Renta Taught Me

I'd like to share an example of a person who epitomizes following the Six Steps to Wealth—clothing designer Oscar de la Renta. I was so sad when he passed away at age eighty-two. I felt a special connection to Oscar because on my honeymoon we stayed the Punta Cana Resort and Club in the Dominican Republic, a hotel he decorated to the nines on the island where he was born and raised. The hotel was spectacular and so tasteful—bright and cheery yet elegant and refined. It was like a Ritz Carlton combined with a couture gown. Oscar had the quintessential touch for design.

The fortune Oscar amassed during his lifetime was reportedly over $100 million. Let's see how his story fits the Six Steps to Wealth:

As a boy, he dreamed of being a painter. Step One: Create a Wealthy Mindset by visualizing what's possible for you and believing you can do it.

He saved his money—Step Two: Save a Nest Egg—and moved to Spain. While studying at the Academy of San Fernando in Madrid, he was mesmerized by the fashion world and started sketching for leading Spanish fashion houses. Eventually, he became an apprentice to Balenciaga, then moved to Paris as a couture assistant at Lanvin— Step Three: Find a Mentor.

After moving to New York, he worked for Elizabeth Arden for two years before launching his own collection in 1965. Step Four: Invest in a Money Engine—starting a business is how 77 percent of the wealthy create their wealth. He dressed First Lady Jacqueline Kennedy, film stars, and royalty. Step Five: Compound at a High Rate.

He then diversified his business by launching a perfume line in 1977, an accessories line in 2001, and homewares in 2002. Step Six: Protect Your Wealth teaches that diversification is often used to protect the wealth you create.[49]

His story is also a true source of inspiration for anyone wanted to live life to the fullest. This is what I also learned from Oscar:

- *Do what you love.* Always listen to your heart and passion. You are a creator; allow your creativity to flow. Do the things that bring you joy.

- *Believe in yourself.* Have faith and confidence you can achieve your dreams and that your life has a purpose. Appreciate yourself.
- *Realize how unique you are.* It is easy to think you are not special, or gifted, or do not measure up. You are an original work of art. Take care of yourself.
- *It is not too late.* Many successful people made fortune and fame in their fifties and sixties, such as singer Susan Boyle, who first performed professionally at age forty-eight; Dame Judi Dench, who became a household name in her sixties, starring in James Bond movies; Colonel Sanders, who founded Kentucky Fried Chicken at age sixty-five; Mother Teresa; and even Grandma Moses, who began painting at age seventy-six. More about her later. Start today.

The Bottom Line

You can gas up the car, create your itinerary, and pack your bags, but your journey doesn't start until you actually start driving. That is true of the Six Steps to Wealth. It will not happen if you do not try. The biggest mistake I see people make is not trying. The fear of failure is so high. I could have easily not ever invested in individual stocks. I could have let fear win. But I did not and you should not either. Because I have faith that you *can* become rich.

Activate Your Wealth Heiress

1. What is it you would like to do or accomplish but are afraid to try? Write it in your Wealth Heiress journal.

Start small and work up to bigger things. Do not feel like you have to take huge risks or jump in headfirst. You can start small and trade on paper instead of with real money. You can set up an imaginary portfolio and see how you do before investing a single dollar. But do something to get your started. Take one action and move forward.

THE SIX STEPS
TO WEALTH

CHAPTER 6

Step One: Create a Wealthy Mindset

"Thinking positive thoughts and repeating your affirmations is the secret to feeling certain you will achieve your goals."

I often hear statements like the following from first-time listeners of my podcast: "I have been in such a bad place mentally. I have been fighting to change my attitude, but it is so frustrating. I know being positive is necessary for me to achieve what I want in life. But I am stuck."

Here's the truth: Most people really do not want to be negative. They know they need a positive mindset but are struggling with the challenge. Why is that?

There are multiple factors I believe stop you from achieving a positive attitude, which is essential to a wealthy mindset:

- You feel bombarded by external negativity on television, magazines, and movies.
- You do not have a conscious practice to help you think positively daily.
- You tell yourself false stories such as, "You are not good enough to deserve happiness" or "You are going to fail."

All these factors can be addressed, but there is one thing I believe is a game-changer when it comes to developing a positive mindset. Feeling *certain* that you will achieve your goals.

When the book *The Secret* came out years ago, many people started talking about the Law of Attraction. The idea was that creating a vision board and visualizing what you wanted with emotion would cause it to appear in your life. I feel a little differently about it. I am not a big Law of Attraction fan because it did not work for me. But I'll tell you what did.

Years ago, before my husband and I bought a second home near Palm Springs, California, I dreamed of owning a home there. We had vacationed there since I was a child. Anytime I was in California on business, I tried to spend the weekend in Palm Springs. I told my husband I'd like us to buy a second home there, and he agreed. One day we were at an art auction, and I bought a painting for the house I did not own yet. It was large—three by four feet. I did not have an empty wall in our main house, so I had to store it.

Within six months, I found a home in Palm Desert that needed a lot of fixing up. It was a bargain being sold by an estate, and we bought it. I hung the painting in the living room just as I had envisioned. In three years, we tripled our money and also received great rental income from it. My point is that I took action buying the painting for the house as an act of certainty I would own it.

Make Investing Part of Your Life

One important way to feel certainty and have a wealthy mindset is to surround yourself with the right people. As Jim Rohn, motivational speaker and self-help guru, says: "You are the average of the five people you spend the most time with."[50] I believe that whomever you surround yourself with is a critical factor in having a wealthy mindset.

Investing has to become a focused and positive part of your life. Thomas J. Stanley, author of the classic book *The Millionaire Next Door*, said: "On average, millionaires spend significantly more hours per month studying and planning their future investment decisions, as well as managing their current investments, than high-income non-millionaires."[51]

It is true. When I hang out with my multimillionaire friends, some of our time is spent talking about investing—stocks, real estate, and the economy. The conversation is always about possibilities as we encourage one another with what's possible.

We love to share success stories about ourselves, our friends, and things we've read about. "This friend of a friend started selling widgets on Amazon and made $20 million" or "This woman started a makeup line because of her Instagram following and made $2 million" or "I heard one of the early investors in Bitcoin now has $100 million in his investment."

I have other friends who aren't multimillionaires who might talk more about finding their next job or why they do not like their boss. I still love them, but I notice there is a different focus. If you want to become a millionaire, you have to be positively absorbed in your wealthy mindset, and that means hanging with people who have a common belief and passion.

So which comes first—the focus or the money? I say the focus, because the money is in your thoughts before it becomes reality. *Decide and feel certain about your ability to become wealthy.*

Five Days to a Wealthy Mindset

Now, let's put all of this into a concrete five-day plan of action. Are you ready?

Day One: Celebrate Gratitude

One of the important ways to building a wealthy mindset is to feel complete gratitude for what you already have. As Oprah says, "Be thankful for what you have, you will end up having more. If you concentrate on what you do not have, you will never have enough."[52]

Thinking about what you are grateful for shifts your mindset from what's not possible to what *is* possible. It gets you away from thinking what you do *not* want to what you *do* want. It is a subtle but imperative shift.

There is a science behind gratitude that is quite fascinating. Our physical bodies are just molecules that are vibrating. Getting your vibration to a faster level is important for your health and your wealth. Since gratitude increases vibration, focus on giving thanks for what you are grateful for even if it is your dog's eyelashes. That will keep you in a positive mindset.

You must stay in a positive mindset to achieve your goals. If you are not feeling gratitude due to depression or hard times, you are in a lower vibration. It is impossible to feel fear and gratitude at the same time, so focus on gratitude.

Be generous with money. Whatever you give away will come back to you. Give money to charity and the less fortunate monthly. Ten percent of your income is the common goal. When you feel you have enough to give, you feel more abundant. You are signaling to the universe that you have more than enough and can be trusted to do good things for others. In turn, the universe will bless you with more money for your giving.

Give away time or things, and watch the money flow back to you. Focus on how you can help others, not what you can get. If you do that, you will draw money back to you. Money needs to circulate. Trying to hoard money leads to a poverty mindset, which will draw poverty to you.

I have a simple but profound exercise that focuses on gratitude and will start to shift your mindset to attract more money. It is so simple that it is deceiving. You may be tempted to skip it. Do not. What I am showing you is a tried and true method that will make a huge difference in your relationship with money and your ability to have more.

Write a list of one hundred things you are grateful for in your Wealth Heiress journal. My clients who have done this get to about #42 on their list before they realize that it is not *how many* things they are grateful for, but rather feeling *grateful for everything* they have.

Turning your mindset from negative to positive does wondrous things. It helps you see the possibilities that could happen for you. I have had many clients who did not realize they were focusing on the negative when they did this exercise.

Day Two: Decide to Be Rich

Becoming rich and building wealth usually starts with a decision. As Ralph Waldo Emerson said: "Once you make a decision, the Universe conspires to make it happen."[53]

Most people miss this step. Becoming rich takes time, energy, and attention. It doesn't have to be all-consuming, but it does require you to make it a priority. You must make money important. I am not saying make it your god. I am saying that if it is not important to you, you would not have any.

Sometimes, women tell me they do not feel worthy and deserving of wealth. Do you think you have to be superhuman to be worthy and deserving of it? Does money not put food on your table and a roof over your head? Does wealth help charities you want to support? Would the world be a better place if you had more money to do good and help people?

You can have money and be godly and spiritual. You can have money and have integrity and be aligned with your values. You can have money and help others with it.

You *are* worthy and deserving of wealth, and it *is* possible for you to have it. Now make the decision you are going to become wealthy. Decide to be rich.

Day Three: Act as Your Future Wealthy Self

I want your imagination to run wild. You are free to dream the fantasies you have had about money and success. Maybe it involves living in a waterfront mansion, traveling around the world, starting your own foundation, or winning an Academy Award®. Maybe it is all that and more. The sky is the limit. What do you fantasize about having, doing, and being?

Do not worry about *how* you will accomplish it. All you have to do is create the thoughts. Thoughts have energy, and that energy, when focused on repeatedly, creates what we want. Most people do not believe they can have what they want, so they do not even try.

Get busy fantasizing. Who do you want to be in twenty years? What would you look like? What would you own? How would you dress? What would you drive? Where would you live? Who would be with you? What would you be doing for fun? Think big and add a zero.

Now get out of your comfort zone and experience wealth. Go to a luxury department store and imagine you are a billionaire who can afford to buy anything in the store. In my experience, it shifts your thinking. Rather than wanting everything you cannot afford, you will suddenly not want anything because you can afford it all. When the *lack thinking* disappears, your mindset shifts.

Another idea is go to a Bentley dealership and look at cars. Sit in one. How does it feel? Is your subconscious telling you that you cannot afford it? Do not ever tell yourself you cannot afford something. Price is irrelevant right now. Tell yourself it is something you choose not to buy right now. Everything is available to you. Try on jewelry that is expensive. Go to open houses of $5 million homes. Try on a $2,000 outfit or suit (but do not buy it).

I want you to start experiencing expensive things regardless of price. Try them on as if you could buy them. Nothing is out of reach for you.

When I went to the Berkshire Hathaway shareholders meeting in Omaha, Nebraska, you could tour private jets in an airplane hangar. You can bet I toured every one of them. I also tried on a $20-million pink diamond ring. Giving your brain the message *nothing is off limits or too expensive* is an important part of perpetuating a wealthy mindset.

Day Four: Buy Something That Represents Completion

I mentioned the painting I bought before I bought our second home. One of my clients bought her wedding dress before she even met her husband. She met and married him within a year.

Another time I dreamt of having a three-day seminar. I had no plan or organization, just a decision I wanted to do it. I went to Tiffany & Co. and bought a dream book that I decided I would give away at my event one day. Within a year, I hosted the seminar and gave away the gift. The person who won it in the drawing also became my best friend. In this case, I bought a small token of what I would have if I completed my goal, and I did.

Day Five: Surround Yourself with Affirmations

Muhammad Ali was an expert at positive self-talk or what are called affirmations. He repeated positive statements and eventually believed them. He quipped: "I am the greatest. I said that even before I knew I was."[54] If a world champion boxer was telling himself he was great before he knew it or believed it, can *you* see the power of repeating words?

Affirmations are simply statements you want to be true, said before they are true. When you watch an advertisement on TV, it is simply an affirmation that is repeated over and over until you believe it like BMW's tag line of the "Ultimate Driving Machine."[55] They repeat it on commercials until we believe it. *Affirmations are simply commercials to you and will change your thoughts and beliefs from negative to positive.*

Using affirmations does not need to be complex. Here's what I recommend:

1. Write down positive statements as if they are already true. Do not say, "I want to be..." Say, "I am..." The difference between switching from "I want to be" to "I am" is very powerful.
2. Use an already true statement in between each aspiration affirmation. It can be anything about you, your family, friends, possessions, or likes. By interspersing the already true statements, you stop the common problem of your subconscious mind arguing with you. It works like a charm.
3. Repeat as often as possible. The more often you repeat them, the faster you will feel a shift. It usually takes a few days, but you will actually feel the shift happen.

Here's an example of an affirmation exercise:

Affirmation: I have enough money to pay my bills every month and have a lot left over.
Already true statement: My name is Linda.
Affirmation: It is easy for me to invest my money and generate great returns.
Already true statement: I have a red car.
Affirmation: I attract money and abundance flows to me easily and effortlessly.
Already true statement: My dog is named Penny.

As I have mentioned, the book *Think and Grow Rich* had a profound influence on me growing up. I particularly like this quote in it about affirmations: "Repetition of affirmation of orders to your subconscious mind is the only known method of voluntary development of the emotion of faith."[56]

Remember, faith is like certainty. Affirmations are an authentic way to increase your faith, belief, certainty, and confidence.

Staying Focused and Motivated

Along the way, you may run into struggles and doubt. You may have roadblocks and naysayers. Nothing goes smoothly all the time, and that is okay. It is easy to procrastinate and know the things you should do but do not. How many times have you started a diet, and then three hours later you are running to get some chocolate? I have. Literally hours after this great resolve and goal and I have given up.

I am going to review some things that will help.

- The most important tools you have are your thoughts and the certainty with which you hold your vision. Keeping that foremost in your mind is important. The picture that represents you achieving your goal should always be the first place you go when you have doubts. Seeing yourself cross the finish line is important to accomplishing your goals.
- There will be people who do not support you and your goals, which is why I recommend not sharing your goals with many people. Keep them to yourself and maybe a few friends or colleagues, but do not be telling everyone. I have found it dilutes my motivation when I tell others, because I am susceptible to their comments and criticism.
- Some people do not even realize they are slighting your ambitions, and some people purposely do. You have to deflect it without letting it sink into your subconscious. Just visualize it as bouncing off your outer armor into oblivion. Sometimes our own families or spouses can be the ones to doubt our potential accomplishments and us. They say that success is

the best revenge, and I believe that to be true. Do not internalize it. Think of how you will have the last laugh when you reach your finish line and how sheepish they will be sinking back into their pool of negativity and doubt.

- Dance, sing, and smile. When I get distracted from accomplishing my work, I try to raise my vibration, and that usually helps. I listen to "Happy," the song by Pharrell Williams, on my iPod or YouTube. I cannot help but sing along and feel happy, and I usually end up dancing, which is another way to raise your vibration. I also like Pink's version of "Get the Party Started" or Alicia Key's version of "Girl on Fire." You will find your reset and be able to attack work that felt impossible just a few minutes before.

- Dab on some essential oils. Rose oil has the highest vibration according to research I have done.[57] Cleopatra reportedly used it; maybe now you know why.

- Self-care is an important part of keeping your vibration high. Staying away from processed food, junk food, chemicals, and sugar is important. I try not to eat anything from a box or a can, if possible.

- Exercise is also important, although I have to admit it is not my favorite thing to do. I turn on music and dance for twenty or thirty minutes to get my heart rate up. I also walk my dog. If you have a tendency toward depression, these things will help, in my experience. The right food, some exercise, and good music can snap you out of a funk and into a productive day.

- Another wise move is to surround yourself with like-minded people. *Think and Grow Rich* calls it a Master Mind and says: "When a group of individual brains are coordinated and function in harmony, the increased energy created through that alliance becomes available to every individual brain in the group."[58]

The Bottom Line

Developing a wealthy mindset is a discipline. It is a choice you make combined with practices that change the very way you look at yourself and money. The disciplines discussed in this chapter work. Embracing the world with certainty and positivism has been proven by scientists across disciplines to improve how your mind and body function. Applying these same techniques to becoming wealthy is infinitely logical.

You can do this. You can wake up the Wealth Heiress within you to become the millionaire or multimillionaire and achieve your finish line photo. It is up to you, and you already have everything you need. Be confident.

Activate Your Wealth Heiress

1. Pick up your Wealth Heiress journal and write down these five words: "I decide to be rich." Now answer these three critical questions:
   - Why am I worthy and deserving of wealth?
   - What will having wealth help me to accomplish?
   - What good deeds can I achieve by having wealth?
2. Answer these questions in your Wealth Heiress journal. Write whatever first comes to mind without analyzing too much. There is no right or wrong answer.
   - How do you believe wealth is created?
   - Describe the type of people who become wealthy.
   - What do you remember about your parents' experiences with money when you were growing up? Did they fight? Were they spenders or savers? Did they not have enough? Were they very successful?
   - What do you need to become wealthy?
   - Is it possible for you to have everything you want? Why or why not?
   - Who or what is stopping you from having what you want? What can you do about it?

CHAPTER 7

Step Two: Build a Nest Egg

"Opportunity cost is how much money you could have if you had invested the money instead."

Sometimes people say they do not have any money to invest. Is that true for you? Most people find it difficult to tuck away extra money for a nest egg, but it is still necessary to invest.

The best way to do this is to develop some really healthy money habits, which means using multiple strategies to build a nest egg. Pay yourself first. Set spending priorities. Understand opportunity cost. Use good debt and avoid bad debt. Shop smart.

Pay Yourself First

You can start by putting aside 20 percent of your gross income into a separate savings account. This is called paying yourself first. By paying yourself first, you demonstrate you are important and put your goals first. I am giving you a goal of 20 percent, even if you are not able to achieve it today. While a savings rule of thumb is often 10 percent, it is not enough today to get to a comfortable retirement. You have got to save more.

The best way to do this is to have it automatically deducted from your account into a separate savings account. You can also use a monthly bill-paying service to automatically send it to a savings account or have your investment account debit your checking account monthly as if you were paying a bill. Putting your wealth building on autopilot makes savings simple and consistent. You usually do not even notice the money's absence from your checking account.

Resist the temptation to spend any lump sum you may get from a tax refund, bonus, or inheritance instead of setting it aside for your nest egg. You will grow investment wealth a lot faster if you have a decent amount to start with. Sure, take a small slice of the inheritance—no more than 10 percent—and spend it. Use the rest to jumpstart your wealth.

If you already have money to invest—perhaps in a 401(k) plan or other investment account sitting idle in cash mode—consider putting that money to work. Make that nest egg work harder for you now.

Budgets May Be Hazardous to Your Wealth

Some financial experts tout budgeting as necessary for financial freedom. I beg to differ. I think budgets are overrated because they can make you feel like you are on a diet—too restrictive, and you want to stop as soon as you start. Just like most diets do not work long term, budgets are the same way. A healthy eating plan makes more sense to me, just like a healthy spending plan makes sense.

You may feel like splurging just to spite it, creating a bad relationship with money—a feast-or-famine habit. The problem with budgets is that they try to reduce your spending across the board and do not take into account your real priorities. People who are frugal might think they are being really good with money, but they are often looking at the splinter and missing the plank.

Do not get me wrong. Budgeting can be a lifesaver if you are struggling with barely enough income to get by or if you have a lot of debt. But some people are obsessed with budgeting and think that it is what is going to eventually make them financially free.

The truth is that budgeting is not the holy grail and may actually be keeping you stuck unless you understand that you must invest in a money engine to build wealth. Just concentrating on less spending alone is not going to make you wealthy, but it can help you save a nest egg, which is important.

Life is not about going through the motions. It is about living the life you want and creating the environment you want to live in. It is all about the choices you make. Some people have a high income, make poor choices, and feel financially strapped. Others have a modest income, make smart choices, and feel abundant. The choice is yours. In order to change your spending behavior, you need to understand spending priorities, opportunity cost, and debt.

The key is to change from a *spender mindset* to an *investor mindset*. Let me ask you an important question: How would your spending behavior change if you *knew* that every $10,000 you invested would grow into $1 million?

Set Spending Priorities

At the stage in life when you have a nice income, it is important to go beyond having a budget—to set priorities and have a spending philosophy so you are creating the life you really want and spending money where it is important to you.

I want you to consciously prioritize how you want to live and what you want. Where we mess up is when we spend indiscriminately and blow money in ways that do not matter to us. That is called wasting money.

Spending priorities are deciding what you want to spend money on before you spend it so your money goes where you really want it to go instead of being frittered away on things you do not value.

I met a couple that lived in New York City. While both had incomes over $100,000, they couldn't afford to buy a house because they were having a difficult time saving for a down payment. When we looked into the problem, it was because they were in the habit of eating out every day and did not realize how much money was being spent.

The funny thing was they did not value eating out at all. It was a convenience but was not a priority for their money. Buying a home was their priority. They were much happier after they learned to align their spending priorities so they could put money toward their down payment and buy a home.

To develop your spending priorities, think about what you want that you do not currently have. For example, maybe you really want to travel so that becomes a spending priority. You also really want to remodel the kitchen. That also becomes a spending priority. All you are doing at first is identifying your wish list.

Now think about where you are spending money that is not important to you. How about the monthly cable bill? Many people find they only watch a few channels and do not require a cable bill anymore. How about your phone and internet plan? Are you over-paying for what you use? Do you have extra cars? Motorcycles, ATVs, motorhomes, or a boat? How often do you use them? How much do they cost just sitting there?

Here is my list of top ten spending priorities:

1. Home
2. Food
3. Kids
4. Retirement savings
5. College savings
6. Transportation
7. Utilities
8. Insurance
9. Clothing
10. Entertainment

These are the ten basic expenses everyone has. (If you do not have children, then obviously the categories of kids and college savings do not apply.) You must have retirement savings high on your list so you get enough into your retirement account to be able to invest. That is why I have it number four on the list. It cannot be an afterthought that you start to work on after you have saved for everything else.

Let's take a brief detour and talk about the number one priority on the list: your home. I definitely disagree with the idea that you should pay off your house first before saving for retirement. If you pay off your mortgage, you are likely paying off a low interest loan. Your home mortgage is the lowest interest rate banks charge for loans as you are least likely to default on your home because you live there and have a lot of money invested that you would forfeit. You are not getting a lot of bang for your buck by paying off a low interest loan. Also, the money you are using to pay off the mortgage is money you could be investing for retirement.

As I explained, the longer you wait to start investing for retirement, the worse off you will be. Most people cannot afford to pay off their house, save for retirement, and pay for college educations. It is not realistic to think all of those are going to happen simultaneously for most people. I recommend you keep the mortgage. Interest can be itemized so you get a break on your taxes, the interest rate is low, and having a loan increases your rate of return, remember?

A mortgage is also a forced savings account. It worries me to hear Millennials do not want to buy homes and plan on renting. If your loan is $300,000, in thirty years you will have it paid off, and that will be equity. Therefore, whether the home appreciates or not, I like the forced savings you have by paying off your mortgage over time.

If you pay off a debt that is only at 4 percent interest or less and do not start investing until it is paid off, you have made a big mistake. You are paying off cheap debt and delaying your investment savings, making you start later to begin compounding for retirement.

Let's look at what that would do to your retirement account. If you invested $150,000 for thirty years at 10 percent, you would have $2,617,410. But if you waited and started investing ten years later, had the same $150,000, and earned the same 10 percent, you would have only $1,009,124—less than *half* of what you would have had if you started ten years earlier.

So again, I want to make the point of why your retirement fund is higher on the priority list than you may have heard from other experts and where you may have put it yourself. It is crucial to start as early as possible and to invest well. The earlier you start, the easier it will be. Put it off and it is going to really going to set you back.

Understand Opportunity Cost (OC)

Opportunity cost is a business-school concept I learned and put into practice in my own life. I have found it to be one of the most profound things that I have ever learned regarding investing and spending. It is not about being cheap; it is about being smart. OC is one of the things my clients like to learn the most. It is critical for you to understand this concept because most people do not realize that wealth is within their control. Growing wealth today depends upon opportunity cost and our daily habits. Wealth is not dependent on luck, family background, or your genes. *It is the decisions that you make every day with the money that you have that dictate your degree of wealth.*

If you think about money only as something to spend, then you will spend it and end up with no significant net worth. But if you view money as something to invest and grow, you will build wealth.

A great example of OC appeared on one episode of the television show *Sex and the City*. The character Carrie Bradshaw wanted to buy a condo in New York City but did not have enough money saved for a down payment. Later, she realized if she had saved her money instead of spending $40,000 on designer shoes, she would have had enough.[59] Not only that, but let's take Carrie's OC a step further. If she had been able to invest that $40,000 over thirty years at 15 percent, she could have grown that money to $2,648,000. That is the power of understanding OC.

It makes sense to me that if you are careful with your largest purchases and understand the OC of money, you will be a lot closer to your goal of building wealth. Most of us have five areas that may be potentially costing us our future millions of dollars—cars, houses, expensive toys, dining out, and designer shopping.

I call them the five money pits to avoid. If you are smart about how you spend in these five areas, you are getting a good start with your wealth building. If, however, you ignore one or more of these areas, you are not making the right choices for wealth. Again, the choice is yours.

OC and Car Purchases

One common mistake people make is buying new cars and buying them too often—about every four years. Cars are depreciating assets. Once you drive a new car off the sales lot, the value may decline by 18 to 28 percent within a year. By the fifth year, it may have declined as much as 55 to 70 percent. Clearly, a car is not an investment; however, it is one of the largest purchases you will make next to your home. So does it make sense to keep buying an asset that is guaranteed to go down in value and spend tens of thousands of dollars to buy it?

The OC of buying a new $30,000 car every six years is very high. The cost of the total depreciation would be $24,900, or an average annual cost of $4,150. If you invested the money you would have lost in depreciation at 10 percent, it would grow to $682,650 in thirty years.

A new $50,000 car has average annual depreciation of $6,916. If you buy one car every six years, that is six years times five new cars times $6,916 annual depreciation or $207,480 in lost value. The OC is that amount invested at 10 percent annually, which over thirty years would have grown to $3,620,401. Do you see how the large decisions we make such as buying new cars too frequently causes our money to disappear?

How can you avoid this? One recommendation I have is to keep your cars longer than six years. If you do not drive a lot, that may be an option. If you drive a lot of miles annually, I suggest you seriously consider getting one reported by JD Power & Associates to last 250,000 miles or more.

Or consider buying a gently used car. It is one of the easiest and most effective strategies for improving your wealth building. Buy cars that are a few years old, with low miles, and in mint condition. When you buy gently used instead of brand new, you dramatically reduce the rate of depreciation.

Leasing a car is often more expensive than buying. However, there is a new trend becoming popular, which is sharing a car. I have also heard some people have determined taking Uber or Lyft is cheaper than owning a car. Perhaps in the future, a large car purchase will not be necessary, and the money saved can be invested. Viva OC!

Here's an unfortunate example of a couple that wanted to buy an expensive new car with the assets she inherited from her recently deceased father. In 2000, her father left her $50,000 worth of silver. They decided to sell the silver and buy a car. Fast forward to 2011. The value of silver increased at about 24 percent a year for the next eleven years. That $50,000 in silver, had they not spent it, would have grown to $532,854. Therefore, the real cost of buying that car was *half a million dollars*. Ouch.

OC and Houses

One of the most costly mistakes you can make is to buy and sell homes too frequently because there are high costs associated with moving. When my husband and I were trying to decide whether to remodel our home or to buy a new one, here's the calculation I did in my head:

Real estate commissions (6 percent) and closing costs: $60,000
Moving costs: $10,000
Costs to "customize" a new home such as paint, carpet, and lighting: $20,000
Total estimated cost to move: $90,000

I estimated that to move to a new home and get it the way we like would cost us about $90,000. To me, it made more sense not to move and use that $90,000 to remodel the home we already lived in, thus improving our equity position in our home and likely increasing the value of our home. It ended up being a very wise decision.

When choosing your home, it is important to think long term. Many people think with a time horizon of fewer than ten years; you should be thinking twenty years or more. Young married couples often make the mistake of buying an urban condo for a few years and then a few years later buying a home where they can raise their children. When the kids move out, they want a smaller home and then a condo.

Please realize every time you buy and sell a home, you will be throwing away the money that you pay for real estate commissions, moving costs, and remodeling the new home. If you move too frequently, think of all the money you have thrown away and have nothing to show for it. If you spend $90,000 instead of investing it at 10 percent for thirty years, the OC is $1,570,446.

In another example, I knew a couple that worked for a tech company and owned company stock. The stock was a fast grower and worth $2 million. They wanted to buy a larger home so they sold $500,000 worth of stock and paid cash for the house. Four years later, they realized if they had held on to the stock, it would have been worth $4 million. Therefore, the opportunity cost of the house is $4 million. That is what they would have earned if they had left the money invested instead of spending it. Lesson: Never spend your investment money. Let it continue to grow and compound.

Using the concept of opportunity cost is not about being cheap. Even one of the richest men in the world, Warren Buffet, employs the concept of opportunity cost. He reportedly has lived in the same house since 1958 because he understands every dollar he invests in a house is money he cannot invest and grow into future millions in Berkshire Hathaway. He lives by OC.

OC and Toys

Depreciation happens to other items too, not just cars. Things like televisions, electronic equipment, computers, motorcycles, recreational vehicles, snowmobiles, boats, jet skis, and ATVs. I cannot tell you how many times I see people who can barely pay their bills but who have the latest and most expensive big screen television, cellphone, and car—all depreciating assets. They aren't paying attention to the fact that they are frequently buying things that are guaranteed to lose money.

Many of these toys end up parked in the garage more than they get used. If you want to use them, rent them. In the long run, renting is often much less expensive than buying, repairing, and insuring. I am always amazed to see the vast number of boats and yachts parked in marinas on holiday weekends. They cost thousands of dollars, plus costs for insurance, maintenance, and gas, but they sit there unused. If you are not going to enjoy the boat on holidays and weekends, when will you use it? How about chartering a yacht instead?

While you are in wealth accumulation mode, avoid expensive toys or buy them as infrequently as possible. Once you have accumulated the wealth you want, you can decide if you want to buy these things. You will, however, understand the OC of those decisions and, like Warren Buffett, may decide not to spend but to keep on investing.

OC and Dining Out

Eating out in restaurants can be very enjoyable; it is also very expensive. It is fine to have a nice dinner out, but some people use it as a replacement for a private chef and dishwasher. They go out for dinner and spend $150 to $250 without much thought. It is not on their list of spending priorities, so money is being wasted there.

If it is not important to you to eat out, establish a system to help you plan your meals at home. That way you will have money for the things you really value, and your life will be enriched. Every $5,000 spent on restaurant meals this year could be worth $87,247 more in thirty years at 10 percent interest. Again, it is about matching your priorities and money, not about being miserly.

OC and the Celebrity Closet

I already mentioned *Sex and the City* and the episode with the designer shoes costing $40,000 that could have been the down payment on a condo the main character Carrie wanted to buy. What I have noticed is people have a lot of interest in celebrity closets, full of shoes covering a wall and a closet the size of a bedroom. It has become a status symbol to have designer shoes, handbags, and clothes displayed in walk-in closets like a doll collection. Each designer handbag can easily run $1,500 to $20,000 or more, and shoes cost from $500 to $3,500. You might think to pay those prices these women must be very wealthy. Some are; some aren't. More aren't but want to look wealthy. Trying to look wealthy is preventing them from having the wealth that is within their grasp.

One woman I know has collected handbags for years. She has multiple bags from every designer you can imagine, including Chanel, Gucci, Fendi, Prada, and Louis Vuitton, but she never uses them. It is one thing if you make five million a year as a pop singer and percentage-wise your handbag collection is not a lot of your income, but it is another if you earn $90,000. The reality is that women who choose to spend money for designer handbags instead of retirement are doing themselves a huge disservice and may end up broke in their older age.

Every $5,000 you have invested in handbags, clothes, and shoes can add up. The OC of $5,000 at 10 percent over thirty years is $87,247. Multiply that times ten and a $50,000 collection could have an OC of $872,470. Instead of having a whole closet full of designer handbags and shoes, why not just have a few you really use and invest the rest of the money?

I have to say I enjoy watching fashion channels on YouTube. I love a smart shopping haul. Sometimes I wish the women who are shopping and sharing expensive designer hauls were aware of OC. One lovely woman had hauls for Chanel handbags at $5,000 each, shoes that are $850 each, and outfits for $2,000 or more. In the next video, she was buying a brand-new Bentley. I can easily see how that might lead to financial ruin.

I cannot help it, but my brain goes to how much the Bentley and the designer collections will depreciate. It is a disaster that if continued for many years will probably cause the woman financial hardship. It is one thing if you have millions of dollars and are spending the interest on the money on luxury goods. (Though she says they do not have millions.) It is another if it is OC—money that is not being invested in something that is appreciating.

The Results of Changing OC Behavior

Look at what you spend money on and understand there is an opportunity cost for everything. Change a few of your behaviors and build wealth faster.

Let's say you listened to my advice and bought one fewer car, did not move homes, and were a smart shopper. In thirty years at 10 percent:

Saved on one car $50,000: $872,470
Saved $60,000 by not moving homes: $1,046,964
Saved $5,000 on smart shopping: $87,247
Total OC Difference in 30 Years invested
    at 10 percent: $2,006,681

Building wealth is not about being frugal or couponing. It is not about living a meager existence. Rather, life is to be lived large and to the fullest. You can have what you want—traveling, paying for your children's college, having a nice home, and ending with a comfortable retirement where your money lasts. Avoid the common mistakes and you will be much further ahead. It is all about making smart choices.

"Other Peoples' Money"

You may remember hearing the phrase "other people's money" or OPM. An important wealth-building principle is to use OPM to borrow from banks, credit card companies, and individuals and create wealth. Why? Because the way you build wealth is to compound at high rates of return, and debt increases your rate of return.

Let me give you an example. Let's say you buy a home for $100,000 cash (no debt) and it increases in value in a year by $10,000. You have gained $10,000 on a $100,000 investment for a 10 percent annual return.

Compare that to your friend who also bought a home for $100,000 but put 10 percent as a down payment and borrowed 90 percent with a mortgage. The house appreciates by $10,000 in a year. Since they only put down $10,000 and made a $10,000 gain, that is a 100 percent return or ten times more than your return. The significance of this is if you were able to start with only $10,000 to invest and you did that every year, in a little over seven years you would be a millionaire.

The power of compounding is enhanced by leverage and is powerful if you use it for appreciating assets. That is where most people get the concept of debt wrong. They use debt for depreciating assets like clothes, cars, trips, RVs, and other expensive toys that lose value over time.

Here's my point: It is really buying the depreciating assets, not the debt, where you are going wrong. Debt is a powerful tool for wealth building if used correctly. If used incorrectly, it will hurt you. It is time to stop making debt the villain. It is a wealth-building tool and is not bad in and of itself. You can learn more about the difference between good and bad debt in chapter 9.

Other Ways to Build a Nest Egg

Can you think of other ways to find money to invest? For example, I have mentioned the OC of having lots of designer handbags in your closet or sports equipment in your garage can be enormous. Show me a person who has a garage full of dirt bikes, snowmobiles, cars, boats, or jet skis, which are all expensive and depreciating items, and I will show you someone who does not understand why their net worth is not higher.

So why not take your designer handbags to the consignment shop and see if you can make a few hundred or even a thousand dollars selling them? Then reposition the money received into investments that are in the right cycle. That could make a huge difference to your wealth in the future. Repositioning unused items into productive money can prove to be highly lucrative.

As mentioned, another way to build your nest egg is by starting a company or a side hustle. We cover some ideas in chapter 19, and there are many excellent resources out there.

The Bottom Line

If you really want to be wealthy, stop wishing to win the lottery and get a hold of where your dollars are going. You are the only person who can change your financial situation. Think "invest" not "spend," and you will have a better handle on starting to build wealth.

Every dollar has an opportunity cost to it. To build wealth, it is imperative that you become an investor and not just a consumer. Investors become wealthy and keep their wealth, but spenders who do not invest lose their wealth. Which one will you be?

Activate Your Wealth Heiress

1. Answer the following questions about specific spending items in your Wealth Heiress journal:
   - Is this adding joy to my everyday life?
   - How long will I feel joyful about this purchase?
   - Is this a spending priority for me?
   - How will this enhance the quality of my life?
   - Will it extend my life, marriage, health, or self-esteem?
   - What is the opportunity cost of this purchase? Use the calculator at *wealthheiress.com*.
   - Will this keep its intrinsic value and increase in value over time?
   - Is this more important than my kids' college or my retirement?
2. Identify what your financial "sinkholes" are. Where is your money flying out the door in leaps and bounds? Check your credit card statements if you aren't sure.
3. Start researching how you could turn a passion or hobby of yours into an online business. There are people making money in the most surprising and unconventional ways. Open your mind to what's possible and look for others who are having success.

CHAPTER 8

Smart and
Not-So-Smart Spending

*"You can have whatever you want,
but buy it at the right price."*

Congratulations. You won a $20-million lottery!

Are these words you wish you would hear? Do you wish that magically you would win the lottery and have millions of dollars to spend? You are not alone. Having all that money at your disposal would be amazing, wouldn't it? It would solve every money problem you could ever have, right?

Well, not exactly.

That is a common fantasy that often ends in disaster. The problem is when you win money that you did not earn, you do not know how to create more. Often all we know how to do is spend money, which is the same thing as getting rid of it because once you spend it, it is gone. If the things you spend your money on do not create more money, then eventually you will not have any. That is what happens to most lottery winners.

LINDA P. JONES

The Lottery Mindset vs. the Wealth Mindset

Patty had a conversation with her husband. He was fantasizing how great it would be to win the lottery. He told her if he won the lottery, he would buy a new car for every day of the month to drive to work. They wouldn't all be new cars; some would be classics. He would have a huge garage to house his collection.

Of course, you know by now how I feel about buying new cars too often, let alone a car for every day of the month. Oh boy. First comes paying taxes on the money. Then imagine he spent $1 million on cars and $1 million on his air-conditioned, custom-designed garage. He also has to plan for maintenance, insurance, license plates, tabs, gas, and transport of these classic cars. Not cheap. He has now created a whole lot of expense annually.

Maybe I should just lay off and let the guy have his car fantasy. But here's the thing: If he uses the money in this way, I can see where he will run out of money in the not-too-distant future. I know he doesn't love his job that much, so why is he still driving to work? Why is he not thinking about how he could put the money to work and retire? This is what I want to tell him: Instead of spending the money from the lottery, put that money to work to create more money so you have a never-ending source to spend.

Think of it like this. You get a gallon of water annually. Then one day you get a swimming pool full of water. You use more water daily, monthly, and yearly than you used to because you think you have so much more. The problem is that the water is not being renewed. When you empty the pool, the water is all gone. What if you had figured out a way to have a faucet refill the pool constantly so it was always full and refreshed, no matter how much you used up? So it was a faucet full of never-ending water instead of just a pool full?

Professional athletes and actors sometimes run out of money, even Mike Tyson who made $500 million. They make a lot of money for a short period of time, and rather than securing the money, investing it, and creating a faucet, they only have a pool full and soon run out of water. Like the reality show stars who made $10 million and spent it all on private jets, vacations, and partying. They had a good time, but now they really regret squandering the money that could have set them up for life. It might seem like a lot of money, but it is possible to spend it all. It has been done many times.

The idea is to develop good spending and investing habits so you create a portfolio of investments that can become an income stream. Invest it first, and then spend from the income that the investment provides.

Do Not Be a Frugalist

Prioritizing what you want, being smart with your spending, and learning how to stretch your dollars are more important than doing without. There's a movement out there of people who believe it is wise to build a tiny house in your backyard, rent out your main house, not own a car, and save 60 percent of your income. I call people who believe in severe frugality—"frugalists."

It is fine if it is your passion. But if you call that financial freedom, I beg to differ. I believe, like the character in the classic movie *Auntie Mame*, that "Life is a banquet and most poor suckers are starving to death."[60] To me, frugalists are a perfect example of that quote.

I cannot imagine forgoing such pleasures in life such as traveling to foreign countries, savoring an elegant meal, or relaxing on a cruise. Life is to be enjoyed, not to be a slave to money. Building wealth is not about being frugal. It is not about living a meager existence. Rather, life is to be lived large and to the fullest. One way of living life well is to know how to buy quality goods at the right price.

Buy at the Right Price

A wealthy mindset says you can have anything you want if you just buy it at the right price. You could buy what you want on sale or at a lower price online, eBay, a consignment shop, a garage sale, Craigslist, an auction, sample sales, outlet stores, and so on. That is how I get my Jimmy Choo shoes. I buy them for 30 to 50 percent less at the Cabazon outlet.

A woman I know lives in a multimillion-dollar home, owns a Bentley, and had her home decorated by an interior designer featured in *Architectural Digest*. She can afford to shop wherever she likes. Guess where she buys her jewelry? She hops on a plane to Las Vegas and tells the cab driver to take her to the best pawnshop in town. On one of her recent trips, she bought a high-end designer watch encrusted with diamonds. The dealer told her it originally sold for $65,000. She bought it for $2,000.

Think about the differences between the two people who owned the watch. The original owner went into a fancy shop and probably paid $65,000 since watches like that rarely go on sale. Later, that owner fell on hard times and had to pawn it. The second owner could have afforded to pay full price but understood the concept of buying *at the right price* and purchased at a pawnshop.

These two shoppers exemplify quite a difference in attitude about buying luxury items. One paid full price and ultimately proved they did not understand the opportunity cost of that decision. The other could have afforded to pay full price but got what she wanted at a bargain price, thus leaving $63,000 to potentially invest. The difference was their mindset and knowledge about opportunity cost.

I play a game with myself to find ways not to pay retail prices. I shop for what I want in order to select it, but I do not buy it. Then I shop again later to buy it at what I consider to be the right price. Do not be impulsive and buy what you want without shopping around. Be smart about what you spend, or you will spend away your future wealth.

Please do not misunderstand me. This is not about being cheap. It is about setting priorities for how you want to spend money and making sure you are consciously and judiciously spending on things and experiences you really want at the right price.

One woman I know wanted a $2,000 Prada handbag. Instead of buying it from her favorite retail store like she used to, she shopped around. She found a similar bag online at a consignment shop for $400 and was excited to have money left over for her investments.

A Diamond of a Story

Years ago, my late husband proposed to me with a lovely solitaire diamond in a Tiffany setting. I was thrilled, but I also had always envisioned my engagement ring with a solitaire and diamonds on the sides. I knew he did not have a large budget to buy an expensive new setting, so I had to get creative.

Given that part of having a wealthy mindset is to always shop as if price were not a limitation, I asked, "What do I really want?" I finally found the perfect ring I wanted at a jewelry store. It was gorgeous with invisibly set diamonds holding them together without prongs. (Notches were lasered on the undersides of the diamonds.) The diamonds fit intricately into one another and created a lovely sparkle.

There was only one problem: The ring cost $20,000. I knew there was no way my fiancé would agree to that. So I stayed cool and waited for a solution to present itself. One day while visiting with my friend Beth, I noticed her ring featured a band of invisibly set diamonds.

"I love your ring. Where did you get that?" I asked.

"At the Wholesale Jewelry Mart in San Francisco. It is where my wealthy aunt buys her diamonds at wholesale prices."

Hoping it could make my dream engagement ring a reality, I asked, "Can you get me in?" She said she could.

On my next business trip to San Francisco, I brought a photo of the ring I wanted to her jeweler at the Wholesale Jewelry Mart. He reproduced the setting and used better quality diamonds than the ones in the jewelry store. The diamonds were set in 18-karat gold, and once I added my solitaire diamond, the ring looked stunning. The setting only cost $2,000, and the ring itself appraised for $20,000—exactly the same as the ring I saw in the window of the jewelry store.

The moral of this story? I balance what I want today with what I want to invest for tomorrow. I keep one eye on the present and one eye toward the future. You cannot forego today and save every penny for tomorrow, but you also cannot spend everything today and forget tomorrow will come.

Experiences Matter

After my husband passed away, I was so happy that we had taken cruises together rather than putting them off to buy a newer or larger home. We could have easily bought a larger home, but the time we spent together was what meant the most, and I now have those memories to cherish forever.

If we had gotten caught up in buying a bunch of new stuff and then having to work harder to pay for those things, we would not have had the time to enjoy them. I probably would have had a lot of regrets after he passed.

I really think that living with experiences today as well as putting some money away for tomorrow is a really good way to live. I do not have any regrets on how much time we spent together, what we were able to do, or how many of our dreams we were able to accomplish together.

A friend of mine recently read a blog post that I had written about the importance of spending money on experiences rather than things. Her kids had been playing at the house of a friend who had very well-to-do parents and were impressed by the huge television they had. She had planned a weekend at the beach but felt really bad after her kids talked nonstop about this big television. She almost cancelled the beach trip to buy a bigger television for her kids.

But after she read my blog post, she realized things are just things, but the time we spend with our loved ones is what is really important. She felt much better about taking her kids on the trip, and they had a fabulous time. The experiences you have are much more valuable than the things you can buy.

Instead of buying a boat, one of my friends rented a yacht with a captain and had a fabulous vacation. Go on a cruise with loved ones. Celebrate important birthdays in a special way. You will not regret it, but someday you might regret not spending the time on experiences.

The Emotional Factor of Bad Spending

My observation is that sometimes people who have bad spending habits are driven by emotion. They feel a *need* to shop in order to feel better. In order to change your spending habits, you need to take a good look at the emotional drivers that make you act the way you do. Here are some questions to ask:

- Are you spending money because you hate your job and are rewarding yourself with things to keep yourself going?
- Are you spending because you are in an unhappy marriage and it makes you feel better to buy things?
- Do you have guilt about something that is affecting your buying habits?
- Are you spending to spite someone in your life?
- Are you spending like you believe you can have whatever you want even if you cannot afford it?
- Did you have a bad childhood and spend to make yourself feel better?
- Did you grow up feeling deprived and now spend because you feel you can?
- Are you trying to emulate or surpass a successful parent, and spending makes you feel successful?
- Did your past rob you of self-esteem? Do you feel "less than" and want to change?
- Are you spending because you are worried about the future, like losing a job or home?
- Are you worried you will outlive your money so you feel the need to spend now?
- Does spending money make you feel successful?

The Bottom Line

Spending money smartly is key to being a Wealth Heiress. Sometimes we are not conscious of how we are spending. Other times we do not know how to spend smartly using the tricks that the wealthy use to conserve their money so it can be invested to make more money. And other times, we use shopping as a panacea for emotional hurts in the past and present as well as anticipated concerns in the future. You can absolutely change the way you spend money. It is within your power if you become aware, make choices, and act smartly.

Activate Your Wealth Heiress

1. Think about what you would do if you won the lottery. Then think about if you would spend or invest for success. Think ahead a few years. What if the money were all gone? Would you have regrets? Would you do things differently?
2. Get a hobby (like investing) instead of shopping so you have something else to do with your time.
3. Organize your closet so you can see what you already have and wear it more. Remember, you can only wear one pair of pants or shoes at a time. It will take a long time to wear everything in your closet.

CHAPTER 9

Good Debt and Bad Debt

"My own goal is always to
maximize my wealth because the more money
I have, the more options I will have."

Often, people believe that they need to pay off *all debt* before they start a nest egg for investing. Is that a good idea? As you know, debt is when you borrow money from a lender, whether that is a bank, credit card company, other institution, or personal friend.

If you are a responsible person and have a steady income, that is probably not going to cause you too much stress because you have the cash flow to pay the payments on the debt. Stress occurs when you do not have the income to pay the debt or the asset you borrowed to purchase decreases in value. That can cause all kinds of problems.

Having any debt become unpopular after the 2008 recession because asset values on homes declined and people lost their jobs. It was a double whammy. People felt strangled and burdened by the payments. Students who could not find jobs felt the pressure of their loans accumulating. Consumers bought so much stuff in the early 2000s that they had credit card debt up to their eyeballs. So debt became a bad thing, and the campaign to pay off all debt became popular.

17

But is it the right move for you financially? I am going to suggest that it is not, and I'll show you why.

Debt Can Be Good

First, we can all agree that credit is a good thing. Having good credit and access to credit is very helpful. Typically, we have about a month to pay consumer debt off. If we do not, the credit card company charges interest. If the interest rates are high, you definitely want to avoid running up credit card bills. And even low interest on credit for lots of stuff is not a good idea, because you could have been using that money to invest and make money. But what if you used your credit cards to start a business? It might take you a while to get it up and running, but a side business provides an income with which you can build a nest egg. The founders of Google started their business using credit cards.[61] I'd say that was a good use of debt! So if you use a credit card for something that will generate an income, it can be a good thing. Many successful businesses were started with credit cards and bootstrapped. Of course, it is a risk, so you'd better know what you are doing.

Second, debt for a college degree can be a good thing. Studies show that people with college degrees earn an 84 percent higher lifetime income ($2.3 million vs. $1.3 million) than high school graduates, so it can be a worthwhile investment in yourself.[62] Just pay it off as quickly as you can because there is no student loan relief, even with bankruptcy.

Third, do not worry about long-term debt at low interest rates; worry about short-term debt at high interest rates. Long-term debt, like your home mortgage, can be good. If you enjoy a low interest rate, there is no need to rush to pay it off just because it is debt.

However, short-term debt at high interest rates, such as credit card debt, is what should be paid off. Because it is at a high rate, it can double and triple in a short period of time. For example, at 15 percent, a debt balance will double in a little over four years.

Should You Pay Off Your Mortgage?

I am often asked whether or not you should pay off your mortgage. As I mentioned before, the disadvantage of paying off a mortgage is that you do not have use of money for investments.

If your home was worth $400,000 and you paid it off, $400,000 is not available to invest. Let's assume you put down 25 percent or $100,000 and are considering using $300,000 to pay off your mortgage. If you invest it instead of paying off the mortgage, that $300,000 could grow to $1,253,174 in fifteen years and $5,234,820 in thirty years based on a 10 percent return over time in the stock market.

Actually, it is only fair to take into account the interest you would have saved by paying off the fifteen- and thirty-year mortgage. For a fifteen-year mortgage, you would forgo paying interest of $502,604 ($300,000 for fifteen years at 3.5 percent). Subtract the interest you do not have to pay: $951,650 – $502,604 = a net advantage of $449,046. For a thirty-year mortgage, the net savings is $3,018,797 – $842,038 ($300k for thirty years at 3.5 percent) = a net advantage of $2,176,759.

Even calculating interest, it still makes sense not to pay off your mortgage. At 3.5 percent interest, you certainly are earning less than 10 percent. You might even earn substantially better than a 10 percent return in the stock market.

When the cost of money is low, it makes sense to borrow. If we get back to double-digit interest rates, we will wonder why we did not load up on debt at only 3.5 percent. When money is so inexpensive, paying 3.5 percent so we can invest it at a higher rate makes sense.

You can have the best of both worlds if you add a little bit extra to your mortgage payment. You can pay off your mortgage sooner and have an investment fund on the side. One extra payment of 1/12 your loan amount each month makes a difference.

For example, for a $1,200 a month mortgage, 1/12 of that amount is $100. If you add that extra $100 to your $1,200 payment to pay $1,300 a month, in twelve months you would have made one extra payment. It is fairly low cost to do but saves you thousands of dollars in interest and takes about eight years off your mortgage.

Your mortgage is paid off sooner and cheaper, so it is a win-win. If you can afford 2/12 or 1/6 (meaning $200 extra per month paid on your mortgage), you will pay it off even sooner with very little effort or cost.

Am I giving contrary advice about not paying off your mortgage but recommending an extra payment each month? No. The lump-sum payment is what makes the difference. The opportunity cost of investing a lump sum is huge, potentially millions of dollars. So do not use a lump sum to pay off your mortgage, but do make an extra payment each year. That way you have the benefit of good leverage but also have the benefit of paying off your mortgage ahead of time.

The one caveat is housing prices must continue to rise long term. If we have another housing crisis, it will send the value of homes down. Hopefully, over the long term, your home will still be a good investment. There is the one stipulation. If housing prices go down, you may have wished you'd paid off your mortgage.

You may also want to pay off your house if you are near retirement age. Most retirees do not want to continue to have a mortgage. The only problem is if you are age sixty-five, you could live to eighty-five or older, which means you could have been compounding your investment fund an additional twenty years, even if you are taking income from it. Again, the compounding you would receive would likely be more than the interest saved by paying off the mortgage.

Another piece of advice: Do not convert to a fifteen-year mortgage. When you change your mortgage from thirty years to fifteen years, you lock into a higher payment. This can wreak havoc on your monthly cash flow, especially in a recession. There are other ways to save interest and pay your mortgage off sooner without having to pay fees to convert to a fifteen-year mortgage and be locked into paying higher payments.

Finally, roll your line of credit into your first mortgage. A lot of people have a second mortgage (known as a line of credit), which is usually at a higher interest rate. The lowest interest rate will always be on a first mortgage, so if you can roll your line of credit into your first mortgage at a lower, long term rate, that is usually a good idea. Otherwise, because your line of credit is often at a variable rate, your second mortgage's rate will increase when rates begin to increase. If you wait until rates rise to refinance to a first mortgage, rates on the first mortgage will also be higher.

Getting a Handle on Bad Debt

Debt on credit cards is a bad trap because items you buy do not maintain value and you have to pay a high rate of interest. A pair of shoes or a handbag may seem like an exciting splurge, but it's not if you are paying interest on the purchases long after you bought them.

Credit card debt comes from spending money you do not have, which means you are stealing from your future. You are taking money you will be earning tomorrow and spending it today. If your interest is high, it compounds the problem and the amount you owe.

So what is the answer? If you have credit card debt, it is a good idea to just use cash or a debit card. Additionally, you should pay off credit cards with the largest balance first. This will help you two ways. It will help you pay off your worst debt first, and it will help clean up your credit the most at the same time.

The problem with paying off the low balances first is leaving the larger balances until the end prolongs your bad credit score. You need to be cleaning up your credit score and raising it while you are paying down your debt. Attacking your biggest debt will do that; leaving it to the end will not.

Is this worth it? Yes. By paying according to the debt ratio, you will be improving your credit score as you pay off your debt, which will allow you to purchase a home, refinance, or buy an appreciating investment sooner, so you can get your wealth building back on track.

The Emotional Side of Debt

Many people feel emotional about having debt. It makes them worry. They feel exposed to risk if anything goes wrong and they cannot make a payment. Not having debt helps them to sleep better at night. That is why people sometimes want to pay off their mortgage even though financially it is illogical.

You have to know yourself and whether you would rather have less money with no debt or whether you can manage the risk and have more debt. Do what's right for you. Just know that if you want to maximize your money, you may need to take on good debt.

Consumer debt is another story. We talked a little about the emotional side of spending in the last chapter. That is also true about running up credit cards on things you cannot afford. Spending helps us feel good. If there's an emotional pain you are feeling, shopping helps it go away, at least temporarily. Shopping releases chemical endorphins in our body. So does gambling. They give us a rush, a high, but it only lasts a few days.

According to *WomensHealthMag.com*, researchers at Brunel University noted that shopping is associated with increased activity in the left prefrontal cortex, a part of the brain that has been linked to pleasure and positive thinking. Levels of dopamine, a neurotransmitter released during pleasurable experiences, can rise sharply even when you are merely window-shopping.[63]

In another study published in the journal *Neuron*, researchers at MIT, Carnegie Mellon, and Stanford strapped volunteers to a functional MRI machine and showed them photos of products. When shoppers saw something they wanted to buy, a flood of dopamine to the nucleus accumbens—the brain's reward center—lit up their fMRI images like a dashboard. By the way, that part of the brain is also related to addiction.[64]

How else do you explain people who collect items they never use, like a friend of mine whose ex-wife never used thousands of scrapbooking items totaling $30,000? Or expensive designer clothes and shoes that are never worn? Or a high-cost car or motorcycle you really wanted but never drive?

I once read an article about a wealthy man who gave his wife expensive jewelry and said her appreciation lasted only about three days. It inspired me to try an experiment buying an expensive hand-bag. I was excited about it for exactly three days. After that, it was just another purse and not that special. My emotions peaked and then waned. Next time you are excited about a special or long-anticipated purchase, see how long you stay excited after you make the purchase. I'll bet it is about three days for you too.

What could be the emotional reasons why people have debt? I believe it can do with feeling pain in the present, past, or future. While these may sound simplistic, keep in mind these can be deep emotional issues.

Once you know why you are in debt, that is only the first step. It is not enough just to know why; you also need to identify what the right course of action is to change your behavior. Remember, this is at a subconscious level, so you have to address it at a subconscious level to cure it. That is the first step to dumping the debt forever.

The Bottom Line

Debt for education, to start a business, or buy an asset that will go up in value can be good debt. Bad debt is debt used to buy things that go down in value or are consumer items like new cars, clothes, and TV sets. They will be worth less or nothing in the future, but the debt will still be there, so it is not a good use of debt.

Activate Your Wealth Heiress

1. Look at your mortgage statement. What interest rate are you paying? Is it competitive, or should you talk to a mortgage broker about refinancing? Is it a fixed-rate mortgage or a variable-rate mortgage? I recommend only fixed rate mortgages.
2. Calculate paying 1/12 or 2/12 extra on your mortgage payment. How much would each be? Could you afford to tack that amount onto your payment? If you have automatic payments deducted from your checking account, increase the amount you are paying on your mortgage.
3. Check out if you are addicted to the adrenaline burst you get after making a purchase. If you feel the need to shop every week, you may have an unhealthy addiction.

4. If you have credit card debt, keep track of how much you owe, the interest rate on how much you owe, and how much the payments are.

    - Create six columns on a piece of paper positioned horizontally. Column #1: Credit Card Name, #2: Balance, #3: Maximum Credit Limit, #4: Ratio of Debt to Credit, #5: Interest Rate, #6: Minimum Payment. Fill in the rows and columns with your debt information.

    - Column #4 is an easy calculation. Take your debt balance (column #2) divided by maximum credit limit (column #4). For example, let's say you have debt on two credit cards, card A and card B. If you owe $4,000 on card A and it has a credit limit of $10,000 (that is 4,000/10,000 = .4) and on card B you owe $4,000 and it has a credit limit of $5,000 (that is 4000/5000 = .8).

    - Rank the cards with the largest ratios first. In our example, you would rank card B (.8) above card A (.4).

    - Pay more on the card with the largest debt ratio (B = .8) and the minimum on the lower debt ratio card (A = .4). When you lower your credit card ratio to .5 or lower, your credit score will improve. That is just part of the algorithm that credit card companies use.

    - Continue doing this until your debt ratio gets to .5 on your cards. It will take time to complete this, but when you have, go to the last step.

    - Go to column #5 and rank by highest interest rate. Pay more on the card with the highest interest rate and the minimum on the rest, thereby saving money by paying off higher interest cards first.

CHAPTER 10

Step Three: Find a Mentor and Get Knowledgeable

"If you want to reach your goal faster, find someone who has done what you want to accomplish and learn from them."

Early in life, I had a strong belief that if I could learn from other people, I could avoid making the mistakes they did. Maybe this belief came from being the youngest of five kids and watching my older brothers and sisters make mistakes and quietly telling myself not to do the same.

I have had a strong and never-ending thirst for knowledge. I learned about cycles midway through my investment career. I learned about creating a brand and internet marketing after leaving Wall Street and starting my own company. I learned about the needs of women when I engaged in deep conversations with hundreds of women prior to writing this book.

I believe strongly that, to activate your Wealth Heiress, you need to activate her curiosity about money and how it works. The information is out there. Mentors are out there. You just need to find the right ones and commit to your Wealth Heiress.

Mom, My First Mentor

As I mentioned earlier, when I think of who influenced me the most in regard to money, hands down it was my mom. Her actions taught me good habits and concepts about money. When she passed away, she left an estate worth a few million dollars. She outlived my dad by twenty-eight years, and it was directly from her investments and business savvy that she was so financially well off.

Mom wanted to be smart with money and reduce our taxes, so she singlehandedly undertook the construction and management of a ten-unit apartment building. It provided her with a great supplemental income for years. Although she inherited a small pension from my dad and had Social Security benefits, it would not have been much money in retirement.

She managed the apartment building herself until a few years before she passed away. While many of her friends had limited income in retirement, she had a very nice income that allowed her a comfortable retirement and that continued to build her net worth. Although she didn't have long-term care insurance, at the end of her life when she needed full-time care, her income and assets were substantial enough to cover around-the-clock care in her home and later when she required assisted living.

She showed me that you do not have to retire at age sixty-five and reinforced in me the importance of creating additional income streams in retirement and not relying on Social Security or a pension.

Mom had a clear intention to invest for the long term to build wealth. She preferred real estate and was comfortable with it. In addition to providing a great income, the value of the building increased to five times what she paid for it.

She taught me that taking a long term perspective was best. While she owned the apartment building, the economy experienced recessions and bubbles and went from one extreme to the other. She was never swayed to change her investment strategy by what the economy was doing. She ignored the ups and downs of real estate and focused on what she could control—the rents.

Over the years, she also talked about how to reduce taxes. She was always conscious of learning legal ways to reduce income taxes. It helped me learn at a young age that taxes can be adjusted depending on the actions one takes. You can save thousands of dollars a year if you have good tax planning advice and strategies.

Mom was also smart about how she spent money. She usually bought things on sale and rarely paid full price. She taught us there is usually a way to buy at a discount. When you have five kids to feed, sometimes you have to get creative to make money last longer every month.

She was one of the original couponers. I remember her going through newspaper ads and clipping coupons, taking them to the store, and buying multiples of items to save more money. She watched every sale, knew the price of each item she bought, and knew which store had the lowest prices.

Mentors Come from Multiple Sources

Some people think a mentor is someone you need to meet with in person on a regular basis. A mentor does not have to be someone teaching you in such a direct way. A mentor can be a role model, author, blogger, or podcaster.

The crucial thing is to find a mentor who has achieved what you want to accomplish. If you want to be an amazing businesswoman, find a successful entrepreneur, read their book, listen to their podcast, and watch their videos. Let the success other people have inspire you that you can do it.

Warren Buffett said, "The most important investment you can make is in yourself."[65] I completely agree with that. Finding a mentor is part of making the investment in you. It needn't be a large investment—even a book is enough—but you need to start getting a financial education.

Most women outlive their husbands and are going to be making financial decisions they are ill-equipped to make. The best time to learn is when you do not have to. There is a lot of fear around making financial decisions, but the more educated you are, the less fear you will have. Knowledge is the great confidence builder, so move forward gaining knowledge and you will find your fear melting away.

I would be honored to be your wealth mentor and show you what you need to know to build wealth. Some of the concepts are in this book, but I also have special guest interviews and share current news and investing ideas on my website and podcasts. I love hearing that women enjoy my podcast and that it inspires them.

Podcasts are great because you can listen on your schedule. Unlike TV or radio, you're not restricted by a schedule. They are the ultimate educational tool for multitaskers. I listen to podcasts on my phone while I walk the dog and instead of listening to the car radio. Whatever you have to do to make time for your financial education and independence, it is worth it.

Investment Clubs as Knowledge-Builders

I am a fan of investment clubs and hope if you are in one that you use *Investor's Business Daily* as a source of research. I think it should be standard reading for all women who want to build wealth. I have always thought it was way more useful than *The Wall Street Journal*. It will make stock picking so much easier because it tells you which stocks are performing the best.

Delores belonged to an investment club with a group of women. She was a stay-at-home mom who also did charitable work in her spare time. Although she did not earn her own income, she was able to invest with her club so successfully that she grew a small account to over $300,000 and each of her three children inherited $100,000 from her when she passed away. How cool is that? The group invested in Microsoft fairly early since it was based practically in their back-yard, but they also made other good stock selections.

I think investment groups for women are the way to go, and I'd love to see more of them established. Maybe we need a Wealth Heiress Investment Club?

Micro-Lending as Knowledge-Builders

The more women become interested and knowledgeable in investing, the better off the world will be. One example is micro-loans. Micro-loans are tiny loans, often international in location, made for less than $1,000 or even $100. Whether it is buying a cow for more milk or buying beads to make necklaces, it is quite amazing what happens when women are loaned money.

First, they pay it back more reliably than men. Second, they help teach others in the community how to do their craft and make money too, thereby benefiting the economics of the whole area. It is a woman's nature as giving and social beings to help others and organize communities. I know the ripple effect will be tremendous when more women see how fun investing is and how good they are at it. If you are one of the women who are already proficient at investing, you have my admiration.

One of the charities I invest in makes micro-loans online. The name of it is *KIVA.org*. I choose to whom to loan a small amount of money, and when it is paid back, I loan that amount to someone else. I love making loans, helping out, and usually choose women so that they will thrive and help their community prosper.

Working with Financial Advisors and Other Professionals

Of course, you do not have to handle your money yourself; you can always hire a team of advisors to work with you. They are happy to help you. It is wise to put together your own team of professionals. In my view, referrals through word of mouth are still the best way to find a good financial or tax advisor. You can research investment advisors' backgrounds and experience by using the search engine at *brokercheck.FINRA.org*.

You want to start putting together a team of financial professionals for yourself, even if you do not have a lot of money. Getting professional advice is also a good idea even if you know enough to do things on your own. A good financial advisor is worth a lot because you have someone to bounce ideas off, and you have a trained professional to help you with tax, retirement, and estate planning as well as other financial matters. My goal for you is to become knowledgeable and empowered with your finances, not necessarily so you handle them yourself, but so that you know enough to be sure your financial advisor is doing the right things for you. This is very important.

Years ago, we used to rely 100 percent on doctors, but today we are more likely to take health matters into our own hands. We eat organic, take vitamins, and exercise. Now when we go to the doctor, we decide if we want to see a naturopath or traditional doctor. We go online to get health information before and after a doctor's visit. Today we are more informed about the side effects of prescriptions and do more to find natural cures.

Just like how you are taking health into our hands, you need to become knowledgeable about investing and finance. You need to have a sense of whether your financial advisor is making good moves for you. Too many women do not learn anything about investing and are completely reliant on a financial advisor.

It is better for you to work in collaboration with your financial advisor, which means you have to have some investing knowledge. If you have knowledge, you can help make better decisions and provide better oversight. Clients often assume their financial advisors will call them in the event of a steep market drop. If they do not call you, you should call them.

In the end, you need to understand investing because it is important for you to understand what is happening with your money. Relying 100 percent on someone else is not a good idea. You need to be a team player with your financial advisor.

Toward a New Day of Financial Institutions

As I have mentioned, financial institutions historically have not quite understood women. They are trying to fix that, but sometimes they miss the mark. Many financial offices feel like they are trying to appeal only to men. The way most financial offices are decorated—heavy on the leather, dark paneling, and somewhat intimidating atmosphere—do not at all feel like home, even though they are home to *your* money.

How different would it be if women designed the interiors of banks and financial institutions? Here is what I envision: They would be more female-friendly. The furniture wouldn't be dark, but white, bright, stylish, and clean. It would feel like a living room, not a formal office, with comfortable matching chairs and elegant lighting with glam lamps hanging with crystal drops. On the counters, I'd have books of favorite recipes, travel books, and *Town & Country* and *Robb Report* magazines for visualizing your Wealth Heiress. Helpful things would be available like children's toys, a playpen, and a place to change diapers. A dog-friendly area with treats. A lovely bathroom with soaps, fragrances, and personal hygiene products. Tea and coffee served in nice china. A small refrigerator with bottled water.

The people would be different too. For example, in my women's bank, you would be assigned a team of four people: a loan officer, a business banker, a mortgage-loan officer, and a financial advisor. You would be given all their names on one card so you would know who to call for what. You are buying a car; call John for a loan. You are buying a home; call Sally for a loan. You sold a business; call Chris to invest the money.

The message would be very clear both in environment and support. We have created a space that you are comfortable in. We have assigned a team to you because you are valuable to us and we care about you.

Do you like my fantasy? I truly believe that this dream might not be far off if women gain the confidence and knowledge they need to become dominant forces in the financial world.

The Bottom Line

Mentors can be found everywhere, but selecting the right ones takes thought. Make sure that you are connecting with someone who has real-life experience in what you want. If you want to find out more about real estate, make sure the person buys and sells properties. And remember that education can come from many sources:

books, publications, blogs, and podcasts to name a few. At the end of the day, you need to be knowledgeable to chart your own destiny.

Activate Your Wealth Heiress

1. Look at the gaps you have in knowledge you need, and find one mentor in each area, whether it is from a book, podcast, or other source.
2. In your Wealth Heiress journal, write down who is on your financial team. Whom do you have, and whom are you missing? Do you have friends you could ask for a referral?
3. Take a hard look at your financial team. Are they proactively reaching out to you with information and advice? Have a fierce conversation with them about what you want and what you expect.

CHAPTER 11

Step Four: Invest in a Money Engine

"A money engine is any investment that compounds and grows your wealth such as real estate, stocks, bonds, and businesses. There's no one right way."

A money engine is the vehicle that you invest in that compounds and creates wealth for you. It can be investments such as stocks, bonds, commodities, real estate, or your own business. A money engine can be a lot of different things.

I use the term "money engine" because it is a good explanation of what it does.

It is like saying that you want to go from Los Angeles to New York City. Certainly, a plane will get you there the fastest, but you could drive, take an RV, cruise on a motorcycle, or even walk. There are many ways to arrive at your destination. But the money engine you choose will determine how fast you will get there.

Cycles and Money Engines

In looking at the strategies of the richest people in the world, it is apparent that they commit to a money engine based on cycles. For example, in the 1970s and 1980s, it was millionaires and billionaires who profited from the oil industries, precious metals, and agriculture. In the 1980s and early 1990s, it was commercial real estate. In the 1990s, it was more stocks, especially internet and technology stocks. From 2000 to 2018, it was residential real estate.

When you find a money engine that is in the favored cycle, it is like a rising tide that lifts all boats. When the housing market was going up, it did not matter where you bought a house. Some people bought in the areas that soared, such as Las Vegas, Arizona, and California, but real estate around the country went up. During the tech bubble, technology companies were typically increasing in value. Internet companies that had no earnings and profits seemed to go up as soon as their shares became publicly available.

This rising tide pertains to cycles and what's in favor as well as being in the right place at the right time. There is a time when certain investments do well. They change from out of favor and into favor, creating a bubble. Then they peak and move out of favor again. It is something to pay attention to because it helps build your wealth.

To put it simply, most investments do not increase in value forever. They go up in a cycle. We saw that with real estate with the bubble popping in 2007–8; real estate did not continue to go up forever but experienced a sharp pull back. The market recovered substantially, and prices started moving higher again, helped in large part because interest rates stayed so low.

Stocks as Money Engines

If you are not using the power of compounding via the stock market, you are missing out on an important component of wealth building. Since 1986, Microsoft has created thousands of millionaires and even billionaires. In May 1997, Amazon began offering stock to the public. A $3,000 investment at its IPO is now worth over $1 million. Shares in Apple have produced returns of 26 percent for twenty years. It is not only tech companies that are successful. UnitedHealth Group has returned 15 percent for twenty years.

I love this story: A secretary who worked for Abbott Laboratories bought three shares of Abbott stock for $180 in 1935. She never sold a share, even after repeated stock splits, and reinvested all her dividends. When she died, she owned more than 100,000 shares valued at about $7 million.

Although I have mentioned individual stocks a lot, they are not the easiest nor most practical investment. There are a wide variety of investments to choose from. I've mentioned asset allocation and investing across different asset classes in your 401(k). In addition to the usual asset classes of large cap, mid-cap, small cap, international, emerging markets, and short-term bonds, you can add industry-specific funds like real estate investment trusts (REITs), specific countries like India, or sectors like oil and gas through ETFs. It just makes investing easier.

Sectors such as technology, precious metals, commodities, and real estate have more risk because there is no diversification among different businesses. They will tend to fluctuate more and move higher or lower together.

While bonds have the unique situation regarding past performance that I described, the stock market relies heavily on past performance. When you are investing in ETFs, which are invested in index averages, you are trying to mirror long-term average performance, and there is nothing wrong with that. In fact, it has been a good way to invest for a long time.

There will be ups and downs investing in the stock market, but, in my mind, buying ETFs is the right way to go for a long-term investor. It is going to get you to the higher rates of compounding that we have talked a lot about without requiring a lot of effort, time, or trouble on your part. Whether you are a beginner or an investing pro, ETFs make a lot of sense and belong in your portfolio.

Bonds as Money Engines

Remember when we talked about interest rates in a thirty-year cycle? Interest rates peaked in 1982, and they've been coming down for roughly thirty years until 2012. The Federal Reserve has been holding interest rates down, so they have not moved up a whole lot.

But if you follow cycles, they will probably begin to move up over the next several years as we move into a thirty-year cycle of rising rates.

So you have long term bonds with amazing ten- to twenty-year records of double-digit returns, and people want to buy into these bonds. Additionally, they believe bonds do not have as much risk as stocks. People think they are buying a lower-risk asset that will have great growth going forward.

To look at long term bonds as a potential money engine investment, let's go a little deeper and ask why those bonds have double-digit returns. It is because interest rates are so low. That means if thirty-year cycles hold true, you could have potentially a thirty-year cycle where bonds lose value as interest rates increase over the next thirty years.

Looking at the past track record in order to make your investment selection is absolutely not the correct way to go because you cannot possibly duplicate the returns in those bonds from the last thirty years, because interest rates have declined down to nothing. That cannot possibly be duplicated. Therefore, it is impossible that the past track records on these bonds are going to be the same in the future.

Real Estate as Money Engines

Real estate is an important money engine. Since it has been the number one performing asset class of the last eighteen years, the returns have been astounding. Coupled with the higher rates of compounding achieved by using leverage wisely, many millionaires have been created by investing in real estate. To determine if real estate is the right engine, you need to look at cycles, interest rates, supply and demand, trends, and demographics.

Like bonds, real estate performs well when interest rates decline. Low interest rates have definitely been a factor in raising prices of real estate.

Real estate values also depend on supply and demand. When there is too much supply, prices can drop. When there is too much demand, prices can skyrocket. Interest rates impact the affordability of real estate. When interest rates move lower, it is more affordable, and when interest rates rise, it makes the mortgage payment less affordable and can, in the long run, negatively impact the real-estate market. Although real estate is highly local and hard to characterize as one market, it cannot be denied that many real-estate markets have gotten so expensive they are beginning to outprice many buyers' abilities to afford homes. It could be indicating we are near the peak of a cycle.

Your Own Business as a Money Engine

Some people are surprised to hear that businesses are money engines. We tend to think of money engines as stocks, bonds, precious metals, or real estate. Over 70 percent of the wealthy got that way by creating a business. I believe that is because a business allows you to compound at incredible rates, which I am about to show you. I have talked about how it is easier than ever to start a business online and create lifetime income streams. Now I am urging you to call on your Wealth Heiress and get started.

Let's take a look at *Inc.* magazine's list of "5000 Fastest Growing Companies." To make the list, the 5000th company was growing at 40 percent per year, and the fastest company grew at 50,058 percent.[66] Stop thinking about single-digit rates of return and open your mind to the fact that higher—much higher rates—exist, just not in a "no risk" investment like a bank CD or savings account. Here are a few success stories from the list:

Kristen Pumphrey started P.F. Candle after she lost her job and started making soy candles in an amber-colored jar. Her big break came when West Elm picked up the line. It grew from a one-person operation to twenty-five people, and her three-year growth rate was 2,075 percent, which she said validates all the late nights and long hours. She is proud the business was completely bootstrapped, started in a second bedroom without any business degree or experience.[67]

Lauren Stokes did not want to go back to work after giving birth to her first son, so she and her husband started a company clothing company, Lauren James Enterprises. They started with "Keep calm and stay Southern" T-shirts and expanded into other products on their website and Instagram. Now at $13.2 million in revenue, their three-year growth rate is 6,010 percent.[68]

Sarah Kauss wanted to rid the world of plastic bottles, so she came up with a line of stainless-steel water bottles, some of which are covered in Swarovski crystals. After founding her company, S'well, in 2010, she is now the fastest-growing woman-owned business in the country with a three-year growth rate of 3,862 percent and revenues of $99.7 million.[69]

I truly believe entrepreneurship is here to stay. Just like long ago, when most people were farmers, they eventually became office workers and moved into corporations. Now people are leaving corporations to become entrepreneurs. The ability to work from home on a computer and generate enough money for a very good living is still a new concept for a lot of people. I started hiring mentors and learning about it in 2007. The concept of making money while I slept was appealing. So is the idea that through our computers we can market to the whole world. No longer do you have to rely on the location of your store being on a highly trafficked street. Today, the traffic that counts is online, and it's only just beginning.

These stories are inspirational, and the growth rates are astounding. I share these stories with you to show you what is possible. So often we reject an idea because we think it cannot be done or because it has been done before. Certainly, candles and T-shirts are not the most original ideas, yet these women took them and made them their own.

Original ideas are not always the best because they are not tested. It is often better to start a business where one already exists because then you have proof of concept, meaning you know it will work. Every business needs a #1 and a #2 brand. Just think about McDonald's and Burger King, Coke and Pepsi, and Crest and Colgate. You can start a similar brand to an already successful one; it doesn't have to be completely original.

It is never too late to get started to create your own business. Most people still think working for someone else is the only way to make money, when instead there are so many new and exciting ways to make money online. Education may be required, but the internet provides that too. It really is possible to earn extra income by working on a computer at home in your pajamas.

Looking at trends is also important when starting your own business. For example, natural, environmentally friendly, personalization, and local are all trends that we currently are living in as consumers. The three fastest-growing companies, which I just talked about, capitalized on these trends. The founders were looking at the future, not at the past.

What Money Engine Should You Select

Instead of looking in the rearview mirror, here are some questions you need to be asking:

- Where are we now?
- What's coming up?
- What's the cycle that is going to perform the best?
- Where are interest rates?

These are the kinds of things you want to be looking at when making investment decisions and choosing your money engine. You want to be aware of why something performed the way that it did.

So where can you invest now to take advantage of these trends? Again, you want to look at where the market is likely to go, not where we've been. We've had cycles like gold going up very well in the 1970s, oil in the 1980s, stocks in the 1990s, and real estate in the 2000s.

Typically, the next investment cycle comes from something that is been out of favor for a long time and then starts to pick up again. The next cycle is usually something that is under the radar and not everyone is talking about or seeing. As it gets closer to its peak, then the masses begin to see, and it becomes obvious. Everyone jumps in, and then it becomes a peak. The bubble pops, and then we start all over again.

Understanding Diversification

I would like to end this chapter with a few words on diversification, which we will also talk about when discussing step six, protecting your wealth. When I was in the financial industry, we talked about diversification all the time. What was interesting to me when I was reading about my mentors' views on investing was that they were not diversified. In fact, they were concentrated in specific investments.

For example, if they were building their wealth in real estate, then they were 100 percent in real estate. If they were building their wealth in a tech company, then they had most of their assets in that tech company. Coming from my formal training in the financial world, this was an eye-opener.

What I learned is that there is a time to diversify, and that time is *after* you have already created wealth. For example, when Bill Gates made his fortune with Microsoft stock, he kept the stock for a long time. Then once he was the world's richest man, he sold some shares and diversified. He had a plan that went into place that would sell shares on a fixed basis. But until then, he was pretty much all in on Microsoft stock.

I am sharing a principle of wealth building with you. Having said that, I am not saying you should not diversify. Diversifying will lower your risk, especially when investing in the stock market, and, for most people, it makes sense. I just want you to understand it will likely reduce your rate of compounding, but it will also reduce the volatility, and realistically that is a good thing.

But I also know that for wealth building, most of the people I have seen become wealthy were concentrated in a particular money engine. Even Andrew Carnegie, one of the wealthiest men in history, said, "The way to get rich is to put all of your eggs in one basket and then watch that basket."[70]

The Bottom Line

Money engines are your transport to wealth. You can take it slow, or you can take it fast. It all depends on factors like money you have to invest, time you have to invest it, and your willingness to learn, take risks, and make time to build wealth. Understanding cycles and compounding are critical to selection of your money engine.

Activate Your Wealth Heiress

1. Start researching different money engines. In your Wealth Heiress journal, write down what money engines are currently successful and where you think they will be going in the future.
2. Brainstorm three businesses you might like to start. This is an exercise in getting your brain stirred up about possibilities.

CHAPTER 12

Step Five: Compound at a High Rate

*"The key to wealth building is
investing and compounding. Your money
engine and compounding go hand in hand,
and compounding is everything."*

It is really important at this stage that you understand compounding because it is synonymous with wealth building. Let's start with a common story. A financial expert was talking about building wealth, and an audience member asked her what she recommended. The expert's response was that the way to build wealth was to work for it and earn it. I completely disagree. Working for it and earning it will not magically build wealth. Many people work hard and are, unfortunately, living paycheck to paycheck. There is no way that working to earn money is the answer to wealth building.

The correct answer is to have your money working harder for you so that you do not have to work so hard. Remember in the last chapter when we talked about the money engine. The whole point of the money engine is so that your money can do the work. And that is where compounding comes in.

Compounding means that your money earns interest, and the money you earn on your money earns interest. Einstein knew that compound interest was the eighth wonder of the world.[71] It is like magic how your money can multiply at an increased rate. And the more time that you have in regard to compounding money or the higher the rate that you can compound at consistently, the faster you are going to build wealth.

You have learned that you can maximize your compounding rate by taking advantage of the right cycle. I have also talked briefly about the ideas that if you are lacking money (M) and/or running out of years to invest (T), then you have to increase compounding (C) to make up for it. That wealth building formula is covered more deeply in chapter 18.

Thinking Big About Compounding

What about the rate at which you are compounding? If you could improve the rate you are compounding, then you can build wealth very quickly even if you are starting with little to no money.

During times when interest rates are low, people can often get confused about the idea of compounding at a higher rate. I just want to say it is easy to get caught up in thinking small and believing that there is no way to improve your situation. Nothing can be further from the truth. You need to get outside of your comfort zone, and that is where most people get stuck. It may boggle your mind to see the kind of compounding rates I am about to show you.

Let's say you have saved a six-figure nest egg, have twenty years until retirement, and know the right places to invest. If the sun, moon, and stars align for you, here's what's possible: $100,000 × 20 years × 12 percent = $964,629 or if you are able to compound at a higher rate: $100,000 × 20 years × 17 percent = $2,310,559.

If you want to have wealth sooner, you either have to have more money to invest or you have to compound at a higher rate. For example, let's say that you can invest $10,000 annually. With $10,000 compounded at 100 percent, your money would grow to $1 million in about seven years.

I know 100 percent sounds impossible. We are used to seeing two or three percent when we go to the bank. But remember, you have learned about OPM and how using leverage increases your rate of return. Also, I have told you that small businesses often grow at 100 percent per year, at least for the first several years. That is why real estate and small business owners are typically the most common millionaires. It is because they get the higher compounding rate.

I probably would have thought that it was out of my reach too, but my stock portfolio increased 100 percent in one year right at the peak of the bubble. So I have personally experienced a 100 percent rate of return.

Please do not misunderstand me. I am not saying that a 100 percent rate of return is something that is simple or easy. I am simply making the point that when you look at compounding, you really need to understand how compounding works and that it is possible to get to compounding rates that can get you to $1 million.

This is something that you would not see on the news. They're just telling you what is; they're not telling you how it is possible. I want to share with you how it is possible, who has achieved it, and how you might be able to get there too.

A Compounding Calculator

At *wealthheiress.com,* you will find a very useful tool that shows you how different investments work in terms of compounding. This compounding-interest calculator allows you to insert the current principal, years to grow, and interest rate. It also lets you add money each year so you can see what you need to do in terms of additional funding to reach your goal faster.

Let's go through an example. Say you were able to save a $10,000 nest egg, which you compounded at 10 percent over twenty years. Ten thousand invested *once* at 10 percent per year for twenty years equals $67,000.

Now imagine that in addition to your $10,000 nest egg you are able to add $10,000 *each year* for twenty years. What do you think that would look like? Now we are at $697,000. You paid in

$210,000, which was your original $10,000 nest egg, plus twenty years of $10,000 payments. But now you have built it to $697,000. Not bad! You are getting close to your $1 million goal.

Do you see how adding money each year and compounding that additional money makes a huge difference rather than having just the one nest egg you started with? Every $10,000 that you can come up with and continue to invest at 10 percent will get you closer to $1 million.

Now let's look at a second example in which $10,000 is invested at 25 percent. Let's say you want to be a millionaire and you have $10,000 that you are starting with. How long will it take you to become a millionaire at a high rate of compounding, such as 25 percent? A little less than twenty-one years.

I'd like to share another exercise about compounding from one of my favorite real estate authors, Mark O. Haroldsen.[72] He gives you an option of having either one penny per day compounded at 100 percent for thirty-five days or $1,000 per day for 35 days.

Obviously, with the penny, we are going to start out really slow. After eight days, we have $2.55 for the penny compounded at 100 percent versus $8,000 for the $1,000 per day. After sixteen days, the $1,000 per day is now worth $16,000, and the penny compounded at 100 percent is now worth $652.80. Looks like that $1,000 might be the better deal, right?

We now move ahead to twenty-four days, and the story changes. We have $24,000 for the $1,000 per day for twenty-four days. But our little penny has grown to $166,402 in twenty-four days. On the thirty-fifth day, we have $35,000 from the $1,000-per-day investment. But our little penny is not so little any more. It has now grown to $339,456,652.80, or one-third of a billion dollars.

And that, my Wealth Heiress, is the power of compounding.

How did it work? Remember that compounding starts out slowly but then turns into a parabolic curve. We have a lot more money because we are compounding at 100 percent. What this means is that it doesn't matter how much money you start with. If you have enough time and the right interest rate to compound, you can almost become a billionaire.

Let Your Money Continue to Compound

Again, when you are compounding, it is very important that you not withdraw any of the funds so you can let it compound. Once your money is compounding, leave it alone. If you have it in real estate as a long-term investment or if you have it in something that is going to be a long-term cycle, leave it in for the cycle. Give it time to grow, and typically you should allow it to continue to multiply.

The Bottom Line

Compounding equals wealth building. The two are synonymous. Get comfortable with different types of investments and the rate at which they can compound. It is one of the principles of wealth that I want you to really understand.

The rate that you compound at is crucial to your wealth building, and *that* is what is going to create your wealth. The only way to do that is to let it continue to grow in the money engine that you choose. Another principle is that if you can, add money to your nest egg each year, as long as you are not making withdrawals. Additions will get you to your goal even faster.

Activate Your Wealth Heiress

Go to wealthheiress.com and play with the compounding calculator. Start with the size of your nest egg and experiment with compounding rates. Experiment with putting more money in and see what happens. Really start to get a handle on understanding the power of compounding. This is the difference between those who are wealthy and those who are not. They understand compounding.

CHAPTER 13

Step Six: Protect Your Wealth

*"Once you have wealth, you want
to protect it and not lose it."*

In the past steps, we have talked about leverage and using good debt to build your assets faster. We have also talked about focusing on one money engine that will bring in high returns instead of diversifying your portfolio. Diversification while building wealth is not necessarily bad. It will protect your money to some extent. However, in most cases, it will not allow you to build wealth as quickly than if you focused on your best performing money engine.

Once you have created wealth, you need to change strategies in order to protect it. This includes paying off debt and diversifying so you do not lose the wealth you just created. A wealth builder can leverage to build their wealth, but once it is built they need to eliminate leverage to keep and protect their wealth. There's no magic time to do it, but it helps to be aware of a change in cycles. Diversifying can help protect your wealth. It is a defensive measure, not an offensive measure. Additionally, you want to make sure that your money is protected with legal vehicles like wills, trusts, and insurance.

Paying Off Debt and Diversifying

I have seen a lot of money made by leveraging and buying a strong performing investment engine, only to be lost when that investment trend stops. One of the common mistakes made by people who have acquired wealth for the first time is to stay leveraged too long. Leverage is debt, and debt can increase your rate of return as we have discussed, but it can also cause you to lose money faster. You have seen how borrowing can increase your rate of compounding, but debt is a two-edged sword. If you stay leveraged too long and the cycle changes, it can be devastating to remain leveraged.

Here's one example. During the technology bubble, Melanie borrowed on margin, meaning she borrowed against the value of the stocks in her brokerage account to buy more. If stock prices are rising and the value is increasing, there is no problem. However, when stocks decline, if there is not enough equity in the account to pay off or cover the margin debt, the firm can automatically sell stocks in your account and pay it off. If the stock is falling dramatically in price, it can cause a snowball effect where you are forced to sell into a declining market.

Melanie was highly leveraged and made $5 million in her tech portfolio. Her financial advisor suggested she sell some stock to diversify and lock in her gains. She said she was certain the stock would continue to rise and would be worth twice as much in another year or two. She held the stock and kept it margined but was almost wiped out as the price of the stock tanked and she was left with a mere $240,000. Not a pittance, but she had blown the opportunity to retire by losing the $4,660,000.

In another example, Tiffany's husband had a strong desire to become wealthy. He started investing in real estate. As he became successful, he bought more. Soon he had a net worth of $4 million. He borrowed all the equity out of their $1.5-million home so he could buy more. When the real-estate market crashed, the value of all of the homes dropped below what he paid for them. He owed 30 percent more than what the homes were worth. Because he had leveraged their own home, they lost their personal residence.

Staying leveraged too long can be devastating to your wealth.

Wills and Life Insurance

It is important to have a will. As soon as you have a car or a job, you should have a will made. If you die without a will (called "dying intestate"), the state in which you live will determine the allocation of your property. If you are married, have a child, or want to disinherit someone who would otherwise inherit your property, you need a will. Unfortunately, two-thirds of Americans do not have a will. Only 30 percent aged forty-five to fifty-four have a will, and 46 percent aged fifty-five to sixty-four have a will.[73] If you do not have children or many assets and you are okay with your closest blood relatives getting your possessions, you will probably end up okay, but I do not recommend not having a will.

I suggest you see a lawyer or go online to research. States have different rules and taxes, so it is important to find out the laws in your state. If you have children, you will want to appoint a guardian for minor children.

It is a good idea to have an advanced healthcare directive—also known as a living will—to make your wishes known in case of illness or incapacity. You also want a durable power of attorney in place, so you can name someone else to make healthcare decisions in case you are not able to make those decisions yourself. This is important for gay partners to do since many states do not give partners legal rights unless you are married. If your partner were in the hospital, the legal responsibility may fall to a blood relative and not to the partner unless you have a legal document clarifying your wishes.[74]

You want to protect yourself and any businesses you have by making sure your insurance is in order. I believe every young couple should buy a term insurance policy as soon as they are married and buy a home. It is very inexpensive the younger you are, and it can provide an immediate estate in the case of an untimely death. Premiums get more expensive as you age, so it can become prohibitively expensive after age fifty-five. Enough insurance to pay off a mortgage, pay for a child's education, or provide for a surviving spouse are important obligations, and term life insurance is usually the cheapest method to cover the potential loss.

I bought a universal life-insurance policy when I was in my twenties. It was a combination of a money-market interest account and term insurance. I overpay the cost of pure insurance, and the excess earns a guaranteed 4 percent in an attached money market account. The cost of insurance rises every year as I age, and the excess in the money market account helps pay the premium. It is not for everyone, but it worked well for me.

One of the best insurance investments you can make to protect your wealth is a personal umbrella policy. Personal umbrellas provide substantial additional coverage above your auto and homeowner's insurance. For example, if you are sued for $1.5 million due to a car accident and you have a two-million policy, your auto coverage will pay the first $300,000, and your umbrella policy would pay the balance of $1.2 million.

The personal umbrella policy also covers some lawsuits for things like slander, libel, defamation of character, rental property accidents, false arrest, mental anguish, freak accidents, dog bites, and other damages. Umbrella policies for one to five million dollars are common and cost only a few hundred dollars per year, a very smart investment. Be sure to consult your policy and agent for details.

At this point in this book, I have talked in general about many things you should do to build and protect wealth, but you may be wondering about specific challenges you have personally. In the next section, I will address common questions and problems that can stall your wealth building and how you can overcome them to realize your Wealth Heiress.

The Bottom Line

Once you have wealth, you want to take precautions to protect it. It is worse to have had wealth and lost it than never to have had it at all. Once you have achieved a significant net worth, be smart and protect it. You worked hard for it.

Activate Your Wealth Heiress

1. Reduce your debt acquired as soon as you can. Do not stay leveraged too long.
2. Buy insurance coverage to transfer risk. Have a will, durable power of attorney, and healthcare directive drawn up.
3. If you have a large estate, see your attorney and plan to minimize estate taxes.
4. Update your wills every five years or if there is a major life event (marriage, divorce, death, birth, inheritance, business sale, and so on) or a major tax law change.
5. Set up living trusts for any out-of-state real estate so your property will pass to beneficiaries without probate expenses.
6. Consider purchasing long-term care coverage.

EMBRACING INDIVIDUAL CHALLENGES

CHAPTER 14

What If You Do Not Have Enough Time in Your Day?

"Investing doesn't have to take a lot of time. It is like a recipe, mix it up and let it bake."

Women have a lot on their plate. A study conducted by the United Kingdom Office for National Statistics found that women did an average of 40 percent more unpaid work than men, which includes cooking, childcare, and housework.[75]

Your time is valuable. Let's be honest with each other, though. We usually find time to do the things we have to do, like the long list of items to take care of before holidays or vacation. When you really want to get things done, you get them done. As women, we are really good at that.

But sometimes, you do not get to something because you do not really want to do it or you lack interest. Some women put wealth building in that category. It's important to think about investments as a priority. It needs to move to the top of the list to save for retirement, your children's college, or to pay your mortgage. When does it have to get serious enough for you to take seriously? When your financial situation becomes a disaster? In a crisis? Wouldn't you rather take control and reach your financial goals instead of becoming a financial victim? If you're already on top of this, kudos to you. If not, there's no better time like the present.

Investing Is Like Cooking

The big misconception is that managing money takes a lot of time. The truth is that investing is a lot like cooking. The time is spent selecting a recipe, shopping for ingredients, and mixing it all up. Then you put it in the oven and periodically check it until it is done. Most of the time is spent upfront. After that, you are just watching it to make sure it turns out as planned.

I have talked about ETFs being the easiest way to invest in the stock market; they are also the lowest cost. Once you have selected your ETFs, there is not much to do except annually rebalance them back to the original percentages you bought of them. For example, assume you bought five ETFs and put 20 percent of your money in each ETF. If one grew to become 30 percent of your portfolio, you would want to sell off enough to bring it back to 20 percent. That is called rebalancing your portfolio. It is just bringing the percentages back to the original recipe.

To stay updated, I read articles on blogs and financial news sources. I check prices and performance on the black "stocks" app on my iPhone and browse through the articles. You can enter whatever ticker symbols you want, and it will automatically show you articles related to your investments. Once you have selected your investments, after that it is a matter of watching it "bake."

Making Investing Fun

We tend to put more time into what we consider enjoyable and fun. For many women, investing is very rewarding, both mentally and financially. I'm proud to say many women have built multimillion-dollar portfolios or companies. To me, that's very inspiring. If investing is not something you have discovered that you enjoy yet, I encourage you to give it more of your attention. Come to *wealthheir-*

ess.com and see how fascinating building wealth can be. If you feel short on time, I have some ideas to help with that.

Twelve Recommendations to Help with Time

Here are twelve recommendations you can put in place today to give yourself time to become a millionaire.

1. Make wealth building a hobby—a primary hobby. If you currently spend time on other activities like skiing, gardening, wine tasting, reading, quilting, shopping, or even volunteering, put wealth building high on the list.
2. Make wealth building fun. Join an investment club. Get together with other women and talk finance over a great meal.
3. Surround yourself with women who also want to build wealth. Women make time for connections because connections are vital to our well-being. Find some really cool women and hang out with them. They may be people you have not met before or old friends who share your interest.
4. Get your family's support. Have your husband or partner along with your children become more active participants in running the household.
5. Take a course. Get more knowledgeable and see how much you enjoy financial concepts.
6. Hire out work to others. Get a cleaning lady. Find someone else to do chores.
7. Realize that your job will not get you rich. Work hard and work smart, but do not exhaust all your time resources on a job that will not ensure your future.
8. Find an accountability buddy. Have a person in your life who will call you on it if you do not work toward your plan.
9. Keep getting educated via mentors. Please join me for *Be Wealthy & Smart* podcasts on iTunes or Stitcher radio. They are also on my website at *wealthheiress.com*.

10. Keep your Wealth Heiress journal next to your bed. Make sure you write in it and read from it every day. By doing that, you will start to see changes happening faster.
11. Take care of yourself physically. Try to reduce stress, eat well, and move. If your body is run down, you will not be able to find the time for yourself.
12. Truly believe that you are worthy. You are a Wealth Heiress. You need to give yourself the gift of time to accomplish what you need and want. You know how to do it. You know how to make the time. You know when to say yes and when to say no. Now just do it.

The Bottom Line

It is totally within your power to find the time to activate your Wealth Heiress. You can stay on top of your investments easily with fifteen minutes a day or less. Checking in while it is baking keeps you aware of what's happening.

Activate Your Wealth Heiress

1. Pick up a personal finance magazine such as *Kiplinger's* and read it. You will be pleasantly surprised how inspirational, informative, and interesting it is.
2. Put your investments or potential investments in your "stocks" app on your phone so you can follow them closely.
3. Scan through articles on the app daily. Read the ones that catch your eye.

CHAPTER 15

What If You Do Not Have an Interest in Financial Matters?

*"You do not have to be the one to handle the
finances in your household, but you must be
informed about what's going on and why."*

You will either become familiar with financial matters now or you will suffer because of it later. That is not a threat. It is just reality. Did you know according to the Women's Institute for a Secure Retirement 80 percent of men die married and 80 percent of women die single?[76] Also 80 percent of women are likely to be impoverished in retirement, according to a 2016 National Institute on Retirement Security report.[77]

So ladies, the truth is if you do not get involved in the finances early on, you have a very rude awakening ahead. I do not want to see that happen to you.

All I am saying is you have to be informed as to what is going on with your investment accounts as well as your bills. According to Spectrem Group, 56 percent of married couples make their financial decisions jointly, but in 37 percent of households, men make the decisions solely. Women make most of the financial decisions in only 6 percent of households.[78] That is one-third of all households where presumably women aren't involved in the decision-making process at all. They might not be informed or even have knowledge about their financial situation.

It is not wise to delegate 100 percent of money management to a spouse or financial advisor because the decisions about your money are going to impact you the most since you are likely to live longer. If you embrace finances, investing, and money today, you will be more informed and able to make better decisions.

Almost 50 percent of people are most concerned about maintaining their financial position, according to the Spectrum Group.[79] The best way to maintain a standard of living is to keep abreast of what is happening. Reviewing investment statements monthly or quarterly, checking your credit score twice a year, and calculating your net worth annually are important steps to staying informed regarding your financial matters.

What Can Happen If You Are Not in the Know

Since women often outlive men, it is likely you will be the one to have to account for your assets and file an estate tax return. That is the document you complete after your spouse's death. The government wants to know the value of everything your spouse and you own.

Let me share a story: Susie outlived her husband and had to detail all their accounts for the estate tax return. She found out what she did not know while he was alive—he had lost a lot of their money and hadn't told her. She had no idea he was day trading and gambling in the stock market and had heavy losses.

After he was gone and while she was grieving, she found out their investments had dwindled to nothing and she was broke. Imagine the pain and betrayal she felt. It could have been avoided if she had stayed informed as to what was in their investment accounts.

Even if your spouse is a great investor, you still need to be involved because it is likely you will be relying on the finances lasting longer. You are the one likely to be the sole survivor, so you want to keep an eye on your finances.

It is also important for women to get interested in the family finances so you can help make joint decisions, see how your funds are doing, and course-correct if mistakes have been made. Mistakes inevitably happen to everyone. It is all about how you recover and bounce back that matters.

What about instead of being in a victim situation where you find out what happened, you become a partner in your finances and make decisions along the way? That is why I am encouraging you not to just delegate and trust that your financial advisor or spouse is handling everything.

I also believe women's intuition comes in handy when it comes to investing. Here's another story from my archives. Mark came home one day and told his wife, Darci, about an investment opportunity in South America. They could invest in a soda bottling operation and make a fortune. The rate of return was very high, and it would multiply their money quickly. The more Mark talked, the more Darci's intuition told her it was a scam. She talked him out of investing in it, and later they found out the "friend" who told them about the deal embezzled the money. Crisis averted thanks to Darci's involvement.

Why Some Women Are Uninterested in Finance

What is it about finance that makes some women uninterested? I have worked with thousands of women, and the truth is many find financial matters dull and boring. It can also feel overwhelming because women carry so much responsibility around the house that taking on one more task—especially one that could be delegated to their spouse—feels too much to handle. In a nutshell, it seems overwhelming, boring, and something their spouse seems to enjoy handling anyway.

I also think there is a natural tendency for some men to act like the family steward and think they are taking care of their spouse by handling all the finances for them. In my parent's generation, it was not unusual for men to handle the checkbook, and widows did not even know how to write a check. Fortunately, that has changed dramatically.

Today, most women handle their own money, but there still can be a tendency for the man to be the one to deal with the family's financial advisor. It might seem okay for you to delegate your spouse to deal with the money and/or the financial advisor. Here's the problem: if you are likely to be the surviving spouse and you are not up to speed on where the investments are, what the strategy is, how it is managed and other important things, then realize you are about to become 100 percent dependent on either yourself or your financial advisor, if you have one, to make future decisions.

You might find you are kicking yourself, wondering why you didn't have conversations with your spouse about the investments. You may wish they were there to answer questions, or worse, you may feel angry with them after they are gone. It is much easier to get on the same page while they are still alive. In fact, it is imperative that you are on the same page.

All women need to either be well informed about their financial matters or be involved directly. There is no other way that makes sense. The next chapter will give you ideas about how to get on the same page with your partner if you need to know how to approach them about becoming more involved.

The Bottom Line

It is imperative that you are involved in your family's finances. It is okay to delegate some of it, such as the investments, but you still need to be informed and aware of the accounts, balances, and happenings.

Activate Your Wealth Heiress

1. In your Wealth Heiress journal, write down any reasons you have for your past lack of interest in financial matters. What strategies can you put in place to counteract this attitude?
2. If you are not well informed about your finances, get up to speed immediately.
3. Review investment statements monthly or quarterly.

4. Check your credit score twice a year or more frequently if you are repairing it and are going to be applying for a loan, such as a mortgage.
5. Calculate your net worth annually to stay informed regarding your financial matters.

CHAPTER 16

What If Your Spouse, Partner, or Family is an Obstacle?

*"Sometimes, our own families or spouses
can be the ones to doubt our potential
accomplishments and us."*

You love your spouse or partner dearly, but there is friction when it comes to money, so you avoid talking about it. It is uncomfortable, and you just cannot seem to get on the same page. One spouse might be a spender and the other a saver. Or one spouse thinks long term and the other short term.

What about investing? Chances are you came from families that treated money drastically different. Each of you does your own thing with your money. Is there any hope to get on the same page with your finances? Yes. It requires some education, creative thinking, and lots of communication.

Seven Ways to Improve Things with Your Spouse or Partner

Here are seven things you need to do to get on the same page financially with your spouse or partner:

1. *Talk about and get on the same page concerning your long-term goals.* Couples often do not discuss their long-term goals. Where do you see yourself living in twenty years? Do you want a second home? To retire at the beach? To play golf? Ski? If you do not agree on your future vision, it is going to continue to cause problems. If you cannot agree on everything, then agree on what you can agree on and work on compromising on the things you cannot agree on.

2. *Talk openly without making accusations about whether you are a spender or saver.* One spouse is often more "free" with money, and one is more "careful." Which one are you? Talk about why you act this way.

3. *Determine what your priorities are for your money.* What do you value the most? What should be your highest priority? Remember to put your retirement higher up on the list than you normally might want to. It should be right up there after food, shelter, and kids.

4. *Agree to move infrequently.* As we discussed, get on the same page about where you will live. Moving frequently is one of the costliest mistakes you can make.

5. *Allow for "dream" items.* Dream items are those things you absolutely *must* have today. He wants a better set of golf clubs, and you may want a Prada handbag. Have a balanced approach and agree to some spending today, and keep one eye on saving for the long term. One way to be more efficient with more expensive purchases is make them count for your gifts for the whole year, not just an event. For example, use your budget for three holidays (birthday, anniversary, and Christmas or Hanukkah) and combine them. That way you get one nicer $900 gift instead of three $300 gifts.

6. *Understand the difference between how women and men think about investing.* Men are generally pretty comfortable taking risks, and women tend to prefer security. For example, he wants to grow the money; she wants to protect the money. Of course, those are broad generalities and may not be true for your relationship, but opposites do attract, and you may

find yourself with differing opinions about investing. Get them out in the open and find out where you agree, disagree, and can compromise.

7. ***Have a money date night.*** David Bach, the author of *Smart Women Finish Rich*, suggests taking time once a month to have a money date night where you discuss your goals for money and get on the same page.[80] Be careful not to get into an argument, blame them, or lose your temper. This should be a pleasant time where you dream about the future and what you both want. Compromise is key, and so is praising each other for positive behaviors and progress.

Advice on Improving Things with Your Kids

How your family treated money and taught you about it when you were growing up is perhaps the most important, and least talked-about, influence on how much financial success you have had. How did your family impact the way you think about money? What did you learn from them that was positive to pass along? What bad habits did you learn that you want to forget and leave behind?

I learned from my mom that with a little determination you can learn to be a successful investor. Everyone's life is too busy to handle learning about investing, but people who make the time to learn and make investing a priority often end up financially secure. Taking positive action toward your investing goals every day gets you closer to financial independence that will last your whole life.

What are your actions today showing your kids? What is the learning legacy about money that you are passing on?

My parents also taught my siblings and me the value of work. When I was young, I learned I had to work to make money, so I looked for jobs to do around the house instead of asking for handouts or an allowance. It was an important and life-altering lesson to know the difference between working for money and looking for handouts. One creates financial independence while the other creates financial dependence. Teaching your kids to work for money will help make them financially successful.

What are you teaching your kids about work? Do they understand not only from how hard you work, but also from their own efforts? How do you help them with spending priorities?

When your children and partner truly become collaborators in building a family fortune, it will help build a wealth of teaching moments and experiences that can bring you closer together working on shared goals.

The Bottom Line

Being on the same page with your partner is a must. Although it can be uneasy to discuss money at first, it gets easier the more you do it. Take time to really understand their perspective, ask questions, and listen well. And involve your children when it is appropriate so your family is operating as a tight unit with common goals.

Activate Your Wealth Heiress

1. Write in your Wealth Heiress journal where you and your spouse/partner are starting. What conversations have you had about money? Where do you agree and/or disagree?
2. What does your spouse/partner believe about money that you do not? What do you agree on?
3. What are the common future goals you have? Do you both want to retire in a sunny state? Do you agree you will buy a condo? What do you disagree on? How can that be compromised?
4. Write down how you want your children to view money and what actions you will consistently put in place to get there.

CHAPTER 17

What If You Are a Millennial, Gen-Xer, or Baby Boomer?

*"The generations have different
issues. What's true for you might not be true
for your children or grandchildren."*

Each generation has its experiences, challenges, and viewpoints. For example, while Baby Boomers have benefitted from the great real-estate boom over the last sixty years, in some cities, housing prices are out of range for many Millennials to be able to afford. Is renting the answer or should alternative views be considered?

I'll be covering the topics I see as important to each generation and making suggestions how to navigate through them. Although I will start with Baby Boomers, you may want to read through the other age groups that are not yours because there are some ideas that may apply to you no matter what your age, such as having the ability to make charitable contributions to improve the world.

Baby Boomers

For those born between 1946 to 1964, being a Baby Boomer means growing up with parents who experienced the Great Depression and WWII; living during the Vietnam War; exploring new technology like the internet that has changed everything; and experiencing a massive stock-market and real-estate cycle of boom, bust, and second bubble.

Technology Changes Everything

I am a Baby Boomer. In my lifetime, I have experienced business before and after computers were introduced and then having an even more powerful computer in my phone. The internet and social media have made the world much smaller and, in many ways, easier. But I have also learned to be more discerning than ever because of the massive selective information and disinformation online.

I believe the potential is great for massive wealth creation because of the internet, social media, and email. Today I can reach a global audience on my podcast and email list. Marketing has become much easier since you can reach more people less expensively with online advertising and email, but more difficult since everyone will rate your product and comment on what they like and do not like.

That makes the focus on absolutely being the best because being third or fourth best would not get the sale. I think Amazon understood this when they trained their employees on intense customer satisfaction. It is all about happy customers, and if businesses aren't making customers happy, they would not stay in business very long, because product ratings and customer opinions are paramount.

Technology is a powerful tool, yet Baby Boomers were introduced to new technology without much instruction, so there is a vast differential in the comfort level among Baby Boomers. Some are online all the time, active on social media, and spend a lot of time shopping for bargains. Others do not.

In terms of financial advantages, being online offers many cost savings. Sites like *retailmenot.com* offer savings on items from many of your favorite stores. For example, before I buy from Saks Fifth Avenue online, I go to *retailmenot.com* to see if they have a discount code that I can use to save 10 to 30 percent or more on my purchases. You can search for any store and see what special discounts, offers, and codes they are presently running.

There is so much saving that can be done shopping online that if Boomers are not online, they are certainly missing out on bargains, not to mention the convenience of Amazon Prime's free shipping.

Running Out of Time and Money

As I mentioned, Boomers have the challenge of running out of time because they have not been able to save enough, and they are living so much longer. The concern of outliving their money is real. Today the fastest-growing demographic is people living longer than age one hundred. The television program *Today* used to wish centenarians a happy birthday but had to raise the age because there were too many to congratulate on each show. Let that sink in.

If you are going to retire at age sixty-five and live another forty years, are you prepared for that? I do not think most Boomers are. That is a long time to have to provide income, especially with such low interest rates as we have currently.

You are going to have to get creative to find additional sources of income. Even Social Security has raised the retirement age for full benefits from age sixty-five to age sixty-seven, and they will continue to raise it. Eventually we will see a retirement at age seventy and even beyond. Boomers are living so long that the money they are taking out of Social Security is a lot more than they contributed. The younger generations are paying in the money that the Boomers are withdrawing. Something's got to change.

That is why it is important to spend time thinking about creating multiple streams of income that can last your entire lifetime. Creating an online business is a great way for Boomers to continue to generate income into their retirement years. Start working on that now, and reap the benefits for the rest of your life. If you can have both investing and owning a business working for you, you are maximizing your wealth building potential.

Examining Your Lifestyle

I also think retiring to a less expensive city is a trend that will continue. Many Boomers have a lot of equity locked up in their homes. Moving to a smaller home or condo is a good decision, and the extra money you do not spend on your new, smaller home can go toward your retirement savings.

I sold my large home in Medina, Washington, after my husband died, and I moved to our smaller second home in Rancho Mirage, California. It was a huge relief not to have to deal with the high maintenance of taking care of a large house and yard, even though I did not do the work myself. Managing roofers, gardeners, tree trimmers, painters, pest exterminators, pond cleaners, and window washers just got exhausting. Life is much simpler inside of a gated community where the care of the common grounds is part of the homeowner association (HOA) dues.

When you are making decisions about retirement, you and your partner or spouse need to get on the same page. It is surprising to me how many couples have not talked about what they want to do in retirement. Where do you want to live? How do you want to spend your time? Do you want to ski or be near the beach?

I have worked with couples who are not on the same page and do not want to talk about it for fear it will turn into a fight. I say better a fight now than a divorce later. Marriage means compromising to come to an agreement, and so does retirement. You have to talk about what your plans are.

Do you need to live near the grandchildren, or are you okay with living away and visiting? Do you want more than one home and be snowbirds, or do you plan to move to a sunnier climate? What amenities do you want your home to have? Golf? Tennis? Surfing? Bike trails? Dog walks? How active a social life do you want? Do you plan to travel? If so, by plane or recreational vehicle?

Lifestyle questions are crucial for Boomers to answer so they can plan their future, yet it is probably the most unexamined topic in their marriages. Take a weekend to get away, spend time with each other, and talk. No sports or internet, just the two of you talking.

Visualize what your retirement life will entail. Decide where you want to live and what lifestyle you want. It is much easier if you start planning early rather than leaving it up to a talk you have after your last day of work.

Depression after retirement is a real problem because people do not have the social interactions they did at work. They often do not see their work friends ever again, and their circle of friends vastly diminishes after retirement. Self-esteem can drop if there's nowhere to go and nothing to do. You can easily feel like you are not relevant anymore and not contributing to society. Planning and talking can prevent the onset of depression and stop the all-too-common spouse-on-the-couch-all-day-in-front-of-the-television-in-their-pajamas scenario.

If you are single, you have the same thinking and decision-making to do. Where will you live? What is the lifestyle you want? Take some time to really think about what you want to do on a daily basis and where you want to do it. If you want a second home, buying it before you quit work is a good idea so that you can qualify for a mortgage. It is also good to consider applying for a home equity line of credit before you retire so you have it in case of emergency. It is much easier to get a loan while you are employed than after you retire, so plan ahead.

Getting Professional Help

It is a good idea to get a financial advisor who can help you plan for retirement and make decisions. Some advisors have ways to stretch your income. They can help with highly appreciated stock and tax advantages you may not be aware of. Ask friends whom they use as an advisor and see if you can make an appointment to see them. Do not blindly trust the advice you are given but instead verify and get second opinions.

Most financial advisors do not charge for their time. They charge a percentage of your assets under management so they will spend time talking with you at no charge if they think they can win your account and manage your assets.

Spend time finding an advisor you like. There's nothing worse than having your spouse choose a financial advisor you neither like nor trust. Make your selection a mutual decision.

If you are handling the finances and investing for the family, I will give the same advice to you. Make sure your husband or partner is up to speed on what you are doing and why. Having only one spouse handle the finances is going to be a problem someday. If you handle the portfolio, make sure to discuss why you own the investments you do.

I know from firsthand experience unexpected death happens. Be sure your wills and life insurance policies are up to date. It is a good idea to review your wills after major life events like marriage, divorce, the birth of a new baby or grandchild, a major change in the tax law, the sale of a business, a change in health, or an inheritance.

Teaching your kids about money is something you do whether you are trying to or not. They learn from observing and imitating what you do. One of the best things you can do for your kids is be a good role model. Another is sit down with them when they get their first job and go through the new employee packet with them. Get them enrolled in the 401(k) plan immediately, find out what other benefits they have, and explain it all so they understand. It can be overwhelming to start a job and figure out the benefit package, so good parenting is very helpful.

Boomers are members of the sandwich generation, which means they have to deal with college funding and taking care of their aging parents at the same time—plus save for retirement. All three take a large amount of money out of your savings. If your parents have not saved or insured themselves, it can be expensive to care for them, and the responsibility may fall on your shoulders.

Gen Xers

If you were born between 1965 to 1980, you are the first generation of daycare and latchkey kids. More moms worked, and the divorce rate grew, sending many kids back and forth between parental homes. Second marriages and stepfamilies became the norm. You had to take care of yourself at a young age, you saw politicians lie during Watergate, and many parents got laid off from their jobs.

It is said Gen Xers will be the first generation that will not do as well as its parents did. You tend to be more conservative with money, and you are an excellent saver. Having had workaholic parents, you are more into work/life balance. You value experiences over having more things and may even want to retire early and/or take a sabbatical to experience new places.

You would be well served to take advantage of your propensity to save and make sure you also invest. As I have already covered, savings alone will not get you to your goals. You must invest to get higher compounding rates. You may want to look outside of the United States to emerging market countries for faster-growing economies and companies. You are also likely to receive an inheritance from your parents, so make sure you are comfortable with investing so you can maximize your blessing.

You tend to be entrepreneurial anyway, but this is a great time to move forward with developing ideas you have for your own business, pitching for venture capital, and starting or working for tech start-ups. There's great opportunity in the tech companies that are sprouting after the first generation of email, website, and social media applications. What's next is developing your own brand and audience—perhaps on a YouTube channel or Instagram.

You also need to focus on staying healthy since you could live a very long time. There is talk of combining humans and robots, regeneration of limbs, super-healing chambers, free energy for homes and cars, colonies on Mars, flying cars, teleporting, and a host of new technologies. Staying healthy means you may experience one or more things that right now seem like a pipe dream. It will be reality and commonplace for you.

By the time you are middle-aged, robots, artificial intelligence, and energy and space technology will become more mainstream, so there are whole industries that have not even been created yet that will need talented workers.

Even if robots and artificial intelligence mean fewer low-paying jobs, I think overall it will create more jobs. There will be new uses, transition teams, and thought leaders needed. When I was young, they told us computers would be so efficient we would have massive leisure time. The opposite is true. Computers are more efficient, but instead of delegating work to a secretary, managers now are typing the reports and making their airline reservations themselves. Leisure time has become almost nonexistent. I think rather than be a job killer, advances in new technology will create new jobs, uses, and companies.

Millennials

For those born between 1981 to 2000, you've grown up in the digital and social-media age. Y2K, school shootings, and terrorist attacks bred fear and parental protectionism into your upbringing. Victims of divorced families and seeing all the ills in the world, Millennials hope to turn around all the wrongs they see.

You are the best educated so far, but what will the education buy you? You value flexible schedules, free time, and meaningful work. While you tend toward spending versus saving, you also have a goal to retire early.

I recommend you start investing early to maximize the time you have to compound. Remember my examples of how easy it was to accumulate a fortune the more years you have to compound? Put that into practice now. Start saving and investing *now*. Even if you can only invest $25 a month, it will pay off dramatically over your lifetime and make a huge difference. Do the same as soon as your children are born. Start saving from day one.

You are lucky because saving has never been easier due to the apps that are available. I am sure more will be developed, and it will eventually all be automated. Online services like *mint.com* can help you with automatic investing, paying bills, and keeping track of all your accounts in one place. Since ETFs became popular during your lifetime, passive investing trends will likely continue. It is important to watch the expenses connected with the index ETFs and to minimize them.

When it comes to buying a home, you are at a disadvantage because home prices have escalated so much. Millennials may be more interested in renting than buying or even living a more nomadic lifestyle that involves housesitting or other low-cost choices. There's nothing wrong with that, and it can certainly save you money.

While I cannot tell you how much a home will cost in ten years, I can tell you that it is a good forced-savings plan no matter what home prices do. If you borrow $300,000 to buy a home, once you have paid off the mortgage that will no longer be debt but instead will be equity and real wealth in your net worth asset column. Think of any mortgage as a future asset because as you pay off the debt, it becomes equity. If you have decided not to buy a home and just rent, remember it may save you money in the short term, but you will not get the advantage of forced savings and creating an asset.

In the future, owning cars may become rarer as people become comfortable with sharing cars and renting them for specific occasions. This means you'll be able to save significant money since you do not have to pay thousands to buy a car, insure it, or pay for repairs.

One of the smartest investments you can make is to spend a few hundred dollars a year for term life insurance that can be used by your heirs to pay off credit card debt, college debt, mortgage debt, or set up a college fund for kids in the event of your untimely death.

As far as changing the world, there is a special account that can help you with making charitable contributions called a Donor Advised Fund (DAF). It has a terrible name, but it is a wonderful account. When you donate money into your DAF, you get an immediate tax deduction. Then you can donate the money to your favorite IRS-approved charities over time. This allows you to "front-load" your charitable deductions in a high-income year to reduce your taxable income. For example, if you donate $5,000 (the minimum to open a DAF account) into it, you have made a charitable donation for tax purposes. You can then choose to donate a portion or all of it to as many charities as you like, while your assets in the fund grow tax-free. It is like having your own mini-charitable foundation. You choose the charities from your account's website, select a dollar amount to donate, and the administrators will send the check to the charity. It is all online and paperless, perfect for digital wizards like you.

The Bottom Line

No matter in what generation you were born, you have specific challenges that other generations might not. You also have advantages other generations do not.

Activate Your Wealth Heiress

1. Review all the generations and put into action the best ideas for you. Make a checklist in your Wealth Heiress journal.

YOUR
PERSONAL
PLAN

CHAPTER 18

The Wealth Building Formula™

*"Wealth building is simply a function of how
much money you have, what rate you can
compound it at and for how long. Plus having
the certainty of knowing it will happen."*

You have learned the Six Steps to Wealth and how wealth is created. Now we are going to drill down more into compounding and get into specifics. It is going to involve another formula, but it will make a lot of sense. If you are not sure what specifically you need to do to build wealth given your circumstances, money, and age, this is going to answer your questions.

With the Wealth Building Formula™, you are now going to take a closer look at compounding in regard to your personal situation. What I'm about to show you is specifically what you need to do to reach your millionaire goals. You will see how to overcome any challenges you have with wealth building, and by the way, *everyone* has challenges. I want you to know it is possible to overcome your challenges, whatever they may be.

Wealth building in its simplest form can be broken down into a formula made up of three components. I call it the Wealth Building Formula™ or McT. Translated, this is M = Money, c = compounding, and T = Time.

As I have mentioned, my intention with this book is to make things as memorable and clear as possible. That is the reason for the McT formula and why "c" is lowercase. I could have written it "MCT", but that is not very memorable. So the "c" is lowercase, helping you think of it like McDonald's, only McT instead of McD.

That is it. You do not even have to do the math because we are going to use a special calculator for that. So hang in there with me. I am going to take you through this step by step.

M Is for Money

M is the amount of money you have. Maybe you are in debt and so you are starting with a negative number. If that is the case, you need to follow my advice for getting out of debt in chapter 12 so you can achieve financial stability. Without stability, it is not possible to take any risk because you will likely feel frozen and unable to take action for fear of loss. It is better to focus on one thing at a time, like eliminating the debt, rather than trying to get out of debt and invest at the same time. Erase debt first, then you can invest.

Let's start from the place that you do have some money to invest. You do not have to have a lot of money to get started. In fact, it doesn't really matter how much you have. It is more important that you do something. Even making one good decision can change your financial circumstances, so it is important you take action.

When I started investing in stocks, I did not feel I had enough money, and I certainly did not feel like I knew enough. I lacked confidence and was sure I was going to lose money. I was not aware of my Wealth Heiress at all. But over time I was pleasantly surprised how quickly I could recover from mistakes and get back on course. That helped develop my confidence, as did writing down my invest-ment account balance daily. By writing it down, I was monitoring my money closely. Ignoring money is the kiss of death.

You should know your net worth and keep track of the direction it is moving in. What is your net worth, and how do you calculate it? Your net worth is the sum of your assets minus your liabilities.

An asset is everything you own: your house, car, boat, furniture, clothes, investment account, 401(k), IRA, pension, rental properties, stocks, bonds, art, CDs (certificates of deposit), and checking/savings account. It is everything that has a positive value or that you could get money for. Liabilities are debt: credit card debt, student loans, car loans, boat loans, business loans, home mortgage, and so on. It is what you owe.

Add up all your assets. Now add up all your liabilities. Next subtract your liabilities from your assets; that equals your net worth. It looks like this: Assets - Liabilities = Net Worth. Here's an example:

Assets	
Car (resale value, not purchase price)	$10,000
Home (use recent sales of similar homes in the neighborhood)	$300,000
IRA (market value of account)	$25,000
Furniture (resale value, not purchase price)	$5,000
Jewelry (resale value, not purchase price)	$4,000
Clothing (resale value, not purchase price)	$3,000
Checking account	$1,500
Emergency fund	$3,000
Total Assets	**$351,000**
Liabilities	
Mortgage	$125,000
Student loan	$10,000
Credit cards	$7,000
Total Liabilities	**$142,000**
Total Net Worth (Assets – Liabilities or $351,000 – $142,000)= **$209,000**	

Your net worth is $209,000. This is a good number to know because it tells you where you are starting from and how far you have to go to become a millionaire. If you do not know how near or far away you are from achieving your goal of one million dollars, how will you know when you have arrived?

Another important point to understand is that you can impact your net worth. You can increase it by adding assets that can substantially increase in value long term, such as real estate, stocks, art, or a business. The other way to increase your net worth is to pay off any debt. Either one of those actions will increase your net worth.

What will decrease your net worth? Buying assets that depreciate. We have already discussed that cars, motorcycles, motorhomes, three-wheeler ATVs, jet skis, boats, clothing, and furniture are all assets that decline in value over time. While these would be entered in the asset column, every year they will be worth less so they are actually decreasing your net worth. Your best financial decisions will be those that will increase your net worth long term as opposed to a new car that will increase it short term but then depreciate in value each year.

So if you are thinking of buying a new couch, get creative about how to buy quality, but do not spend too much since you realize it is a depreciating asset. For example, you can find a great sale, purchase slightly used, buy online, or order wholesale direct from a furniture maker. Because you are conscious that it is going to depreciate each year, you try to spend less so you have more money to spend on an asset that will increase in value. Then a great idea would be to invest what you save in your investment account.

C Is for Compounding

As I mentioned in Step Five of the Six Steps to Wealth, compounding is wealth building. Compounding is simply growing your money in whatever money engine you choose, whether it is a stock, bond, real estate, art, a business, or other means. It is the interest rate part of the calculation derived from your investment. I have talked about stocks compounding at a much higher rate than a savings account. The benefit of that is you are building wealth faster.

What you are actually doing is taking your income and turning it into an asset that is building wealth for you. You want to have assets on your net worth statement that will grow in value, not depreciate. Looking at the list of assets in the preceding example, there are only two assets that have a chance of increasing in value: the home and the IRA, presuming the IRA is invested in stocks, mutual funds, or ETFs. (An IRA is simply the envelope that investments go in; it is not an investment itself.)

This is key—the more you use your income to buy assets that increase in value, the sooner you will become wealthy.

T Is for Time

Time is the amount of years you have to invest, meaning how many years you can compound your money. Do you have ten or thirty years until retirement? The function of time is important because the longer you can invest, the more you can compound money. It also means the longer your time horizon to invest, the less you have to start with today.

For example, if you have $100,000 and only ten years to invest, at 10 percent your money will grow to $259,374. But if you have the same amount of money and thirty years to invest it, at 10 percent it will grow to $1,744,940. Quite a difference.

Having more time means you have more years to allow the magic of compounding to work for you. That is why it is extremely important to start investing as soon as possible.

Planning Using the McT Formula

Many people are missing one or more parts of the wealth building McT (Money × compounding × Time) formula. Once you comprehend the formula, the magic is not in the formula itself as much as it is your internalization and comprehension of your shortcomings. Once you understand where you have the greatest weaknesses and close those gaps, you will start to make great progress.

Not having many years left until you retire, not having much money to invest, and making the right investments are all very different issues. Yet all three are crucial in determining how much you are going to have when you retire.

Since they all work together, a shortage of one or more is going to provide obstacles for you to overcome, making it more difficult or delaying your ability to reach your goal. You can, however, still become a millionaire by making some adjustments.

People usually have at least one of the following limitations that make it challenging to build wealth and reach a goal of one million dollars:

- *Not enough money to start.* Your retirement accounts and other savings do not come close to $100,000 or more to invest.
- *Not enough time (years)* to grow your wealth, even though you have a nice nest egg. Your investments got a late start, and you do not have many years until retirement. If you have fewer than ten years to grow your wealth, it can be a challenge.
- *Not enough compounding.* You have a good nest egg saved and more than ten years until retirement, but your investments are compounding at 2 percent or less.
- *Not enough knowledge.* You do not know where or how to invest in order to create the wealth you want.
- *Not enough certainty that you can do it.* I find people do not even try because they do not believe they can really become a millionaire.

The solution is to have a personal plan. Your Millionaire Action Plan (MAP)™ will help you set goals and put a plan in place. The MAP™ gives you a plan to follow no matter where you are right now and helps you overcome any shortcomings you may have in any of these areas.

The Bottom Line

Understanding how wealth building works makes it much easier to realize your goals. Once again, make sure you are familiar with the three parts of the Wealth Building Formula™ and what "McT" means.

Activate Your Wealth Heiress

1. Calculate your net worth and then look at your assets. Have you been naturally doing a good job of acquiring assets that can appreciate or are you spending the majority of your money on assets that depreciate? What action can you take to improve?
2. In your Wealth Heiress journal, review the limitations you have with the McT formula. Clearly articulate issues around money, compounding, and time.

CHAPTER 19

Your Own Millionaire Action Plan (MAP)™

*"Do not feel discouraged if you do not think
you are on track or it seems impossible. Nothing
is impossible because you are a Wealth Heiress."*

You have made it through everything you need to know to develop your Millionaire Action Plan (MAP)™. You have learned how the Wealth Building Formula™ (McT) works. You know if you lack one or more components, you need to make it up by increasing another.

The Millionaire Action Plan (MAP)™ is not a financial plan. It is a tool that pulls all the thinking together in a thoughtful way so you know what to do next and where to focus. It also enables you to course-correct in case you are off-target.

Putting Your Millionaire Action Plan (MAP)™ to Work

Get out your Wealth Heiress journal, iPad, or some pen and paper, and write down your answers and actions for the next eleven components that make up your (MAP)™. Do not skip any since they are all important.

1. Let's start with the net worth you calculated last chapter. Take only the assets from your net worth that can compound and list them. Ignore assets that do not appreciate. For example, assets like real estate (minus any mortgage), stocks, cash, an IRA and 401(k) invested in mutual funds, and a bond can all appreciate. Jewelry, cars, and a boat won't appreciate, so ignore them in the MAP™.

2. Determine how many years remaining until you want to achieve your goal.

3. Using the Wealth Building Formula™ (McT), decide the one you are lacking the most: money, time, or compounding rate.

4. Decide the one you can improve the most—M, c, or T?

5. Take your total assets from question one, and calculate when you will become a millionaire using the calculator at *wealthheiress.com*.

6. Experiment using different compounding rates.

7. Using the (McT) formula, what do you plan to change? Can you move money from a lower compounding asset to a higher rate of compounding asset? For example, can you take $10,000 in cash inside your 401(k) and invest it in a mutual fund?

8. Select the money engines you are planning to use to achieve your goal. List them and add specific details of how you will do this.

9. Determine what you need to do to prepare to invest in the money engines. For example, get more education, look at rental houses, research starting a business, investigate ETFs, and so forth.

10. Break your answers to question eight into smaller actions, such as making a phone call, researching online, or reading a book.

11. Write your "finish line" vision (mental picture) for yourself. Describe in detail what it will look like when you achieve your goal.

12. Determine how you can you keep that picture in your mind and increase the certainty you will achieve it.

Let's take a look at two examples so you can see how it works.

Anna starts with the total of her assets that can compound—401(k) at $230,000, a variable annuity at $60,000, and IRAs at $119,000 to total $409,000. She wants to retire in seventeen years. She calculates the amount at retirement: $409,000 × 17 years × 10 percent (factor computed by calculator) = $2,067,278. She determines that she is in pretty good shape for retirement, assuming the stock market provides historical returns.

Jane starts with the total of her retirement contributions at $105,000, which is significantly less than Anna. Jane also wants to retire in seventeen years and sets a factor of 10 percent for the compounding rate, or $105,000 × 17 × 10 percent (factor computed by calculator) = $530,719. Jane will not have enough to retire.

Her options are to increase the money (M) saved, lengthen the years (T), and/or improve the rate of compounding (c). To improve M, she needs to go back to solutions to get more money, like saving more, selling things, getting a second job, or starting a business. To improve T, she needs to consider retiring a few years later. Instead of retiring at age sixty-five, Jane could retire at age sixty-eight, giving her three more years to compound. To improve c, she needs to invest in the next cycle so she can improve her rate of return.

Other Examples of Millionaire Action Plan (MAP)s™

The following are scenarios of other MAPs™ so you can see the wide variety of situations and options.

- Barbara was out of the work force raising kids for twenty years and went back to work as a manager at age fifty. She wanted to retire at age sixty-five, but since she was short on years until retirement (T), she knew she had to either increase the money (M), set aside or compound (c) at a higher rate, or both. Because she was age fifty, she took advantage the maximum 401(k) contribution of $18,500 plus the additional $6,000 allowed as a "catch-up provision" and put $24,500 into her 401(k). Her employer also matched four percent of her contributions per year, or $980. Her contribution and match equaled $25,480 annually, and in fifteen years at 10 percent, her retirement fund grew to $996,955.

- Karen was a successful real-estate agent. She started saving and buying rental houses, putting 20 percent down and borrowing the rest. She would take out the equity and buy another house. Soon she owned five homes that were rented and paying for themselves. Her initial $50,000 investment averaged 30 percent and grew to $2.5 million in fifteen years.

- Ashley and Karen wanted to become millionaires. Both reached their goals, but the amount required to get there varied drastically. Karen started saving for retirement at age forty-five and had to save $20,400 annually in order to become a millionaire. Ashley started saving at age twenty-five, and since she had more time (T) to compound, she only had to save $3,445 per year.

- Christie went to work for a tech company. Tech companies have had above average returns (c) on their stock, and many stockholders have become millionaires. She started investing $9,000 annually at age forty-five and averaged 15 percent for twenty years, accumulating $1,041,078 by age sixty-five.

- Brianna was a masseuse and was hired to work for a high-tech company as a perk for their employees at $450 a week. Rather than take her pay in cash, she asked if she could have some stock options instead. Five years later when the company went public, the stock went from $85 to over $700 and was worth more than a million dollars. Now she has her own masseuse.

- Whitney is a twenty-five-year-old social media entrepreneur who is starting her own company. She invests $25 a month. If she earns 10 percent per year, by age sixty-five she will have $640,000. If she waits until age forty, she'll have to save $475 per month for it to grow to the same amount. At twenty-five, her total investment is $48,000, and if she waits until forty, her total investment would be $142,000.

- Sara spent her spare time investing in stocks. Over time, it really added up due to the compounding (c). She never made more than $11 per hour but accumulated more than $3,000,000 in her lifetime. She religiously invested $500 every month and had a portfolio of stocks that performed extremely well. Investing $6,000 annually for twenty-five years at 19 percent became $3,334,911.

Strategies Around Money and Time

If you are frustrated by the lack of money saved, do not despair. A lot of people do not have enough money saved for retirement. It has become a national crisis in America. Women have a more difficult time than men because we have a double whammy.

First, we live longer than men. Women actually need more money than men, yet we have less. Life expectancy for women is 82.9 years and 79.2 years for men. Additionally, more than one in three sixty-five year olds today will live to ninety, and more than one in seven will live to age ninety-five.[81]

Second, we have not saved enough. I think there are many reasons why women are in this boat, such as lacking a financial education; lacking savings and investment; limitations on retirement contributions, earning only 80 percent of what men make; and leaving the workforce during child-raising years. The bottom line is not enough money is saved early enough.

Accumulating wealth is also a problem of time. The earlier you start, the less it takes to build wealth, and so time is an important part of the equation. That is why I believe it is imperative we get people started investing in their twenties.

For example, if you started investing $18,500 in your 401(k) per year for thirty years, it would grow to $3,670,267. If you invested $18,500 per year, but started ten years later, it would only grow to $1,290,004. And if you invested the $18,500 per year but started twenty years later, it would only grow to $372,310.

Opening an IRA and starting your investment program while you are young is the best thing you can do for your retirement. The ideal scenario is starting to save early because it puts time on your side so you have long periods of time to compound. Having thirty years to compound money makes a big difference.

Not having enough money to retire often means you are running out of time (T) to compound your money. Fortunately, there is what's called a "catch-up provision" in your 401(k), which allows people over age fifty to contribute an additional $6,000, $24,500 annually, to help save more for retirement. Let's see how that can help your retirement account if you take advantage of it.

If you are fifty years old and contribute $18,500 per year into your 401(k), at 10 percent annually, that could grow to $723,849 by age sixty-five. But if you add $6,000 per year, then $24,500 per year at 10 percent could grow to $958,610, an additional $234,761 by investing an additional $90,000 (15 × $6,000). It is worth it to take advantage of the catch-up provision. Just like all 401(k) contributions, you are not taxed on the income, and it grows without tax too.

Another way people are choosing to fix the running-out-of-time problem is to delay retirement a few years. Interestingly, more Baby Boomers are declaring they never plan to retire. You certainly can choose to work for the rest of your life if you want to, but being a ninety year old greeter at Walmart probably isn't what you have in mind.

It is okay to delay retirement if that is what you want, but I do not think that is what many people want. They do not have a retirement income other than Social Security, which for most people is not enough if it's their sole source of support. According to Investopedia, the estimated average monthly benefit for "all retired workers" in 2016 was $1,341.[82] Clearly, more income is necessary for a comfortable retirement and healthcare needs in your elderly years.

Automatic Savings

If you do not have a lot of money in savings or investments, it means you are going to have to save or earn more to make up for the money that is lacking. One of the best things you can do is save money like you are paying a bill—even better if you have it automatically deducted from your bank account. Warren Buffett said, "Do not save what is left after spending, but spend what is left after saving."[83] Our Wealth Heiress target savings rate is 20 percent annually, meaning you should be saving 20 percent or more of your income. If you can't save that much, then save as close to 20 percent as you can.

You can certainly use micro-saving service apps to help you save more. The Acorns app helps you save your spare change by rounding up a purchase and using it to go to your investment account. Let's say you buy a cup of coffee for $2.30. The app will round that amount up to three dollars and move 70 cents into your account. You can choose to round up or set a fixed amount so your investment account grows faster.

The Digit app will determine how much you should be saving based on your income and spending and then automatically save it for you. You pay fees for these savings apps, so be aware you are paying for the convenience. If you are disciplined enough to save without them, that is even better.

A service I've long recommended is setting up a $100-a-month (higher if possible) automatic deduction with a mutual fund company. You will not be charged for what you save, just a small percentage of the assets under management. It comes right out of your checking account and buys shares in a mutual fund. As soon as you, your children, or grandchildren have a job, you should be doing this in addition to your 401(k) contributions.

Max out your 401(k) first because you often get free money if your employer matches your contribution (usually up to a percentage match) plus you are not taxed on the money that goes into your 401(k). So if you earn $50,000 and $2,000 goes into your 401(k), then you will only pay tax on $48,000 of income earned, plus the employer's match goes into your account and is not taxed until it is time to take the money out.

Earn More Money

Another option is to earn more money. If you have a job, your raises are probably limited, so it is going to have to come from somewhere else. Fortunately, because of the internet, there are all kinds of ways to make money that did not exist before.

Today there are many jobs with flexible hours, which make it easy to plan around your primary job. Whether you decide to drive for Uber, Lyft, offer your handy services on *taskrabbit.com*, be a barista, or something else, generating additional income so you can save more money is imperative. Old-fashioned businesses like window washing, painting, gardening, baking, housesitting, dog sitting, and dog walking are tried-and-true income generators. Some dog walkers make $100,000 annually.[84]

Abby was $30,000 in debt. She was working as a Pilates instructor. I asked her if she had any way to make more money or any side skills? She said she used to be a fitness model. I suggested she look into getting modeling gigs. She also had a spare bedroom in her apartment, which I suggested she rent out. She followed through on both of my suggestions and paid off all her debt in six months.

Sadie, a seventy-year-old woman who worked in a church for thirty years, just found out there was not enough money in the pension and she would not be receiving income she had counted on for retirement. She did not have much in savings, so she has to rely on Social Security for income. To reduce expenses, she moved in with her son and daughter-in-law. Is it too late for her? No, she can get a computer and take lessons on *lynda.com* to improve her business, computer, or creative skills and train in a new career working from home. She could expand her options to become a virtual assistant or use other money-making strategies mentioned in this book. There are many well-paying online careers available today that did not exist even a few years ago—and your age or location doesn't matter. Get savvy with technology and expand your thinking.

Get out of the mindset that you need another job to make money. There are many new ways to create income than ever before. This is the era of prosperity, but some people can't see it yet. It is like you are in a grocery store and you are worried you are going to starve to death. There are more ways to make money online than we ever had before. It requires you to start studying and learning how, but it is possible to make a lot of money with a computer and some know-how.

Become a Merchant

Go through your garage, closets, and spare rooms, and have a big garage sale. You can also sell your designer shoes, handbags and clothes on *poshmark.com* and sell jeans and casual clothes at *letgo.com*. Get rid of anything you have not worn in two years. Old golf clubs, bikes, extra cars, boats, motorcycles, and three-wheelers are also good candidates to sell.

You can put local ads on Craigslist, *Offerup.com*, or on a local Facebook page in your community. People can pick up them up locally so you do not have to worry about shipping large items. A friend of mine did this with a twenty-year-old washer and dryer set that most of us would assume were worth nothing. She sold them locally for $500 each.

Sell your CDs, DVDs, Blu-ray discs, video games, old phones, and iPads on decluttr.com for $1-plus each. Sell your used books on Amazon. Also scan eBay to see what is selling and at what price. You'll be amazed that what you formerly thought was junk is some-one else's diamond.

Cottage businesses are springing up with people scouring garage sales for baseball cards, books, and toys and selling them on *amazon.com* or selling designer brands found at Goodwill and consignment shops at *Poshmark.com*.

Katrina sells baseball cards, old legal documents, dolls, and the hottest Christmas toys on her eBay and *Shopify.com* stores. Sometimes she buys toys at Walmart and resells them on eBay, especially if there is a shortage of a popular toy in retail stores. Buyers bid up the prices of the toys, and she makes a solid profit.

You can even become a retailer on *shopify.com* and set up a shop sourcing your goods from *alibaba.com*. They ship for you, and you collect the money. Many entrepreneurs are buying goods wholesale and reselling them on *amazon.com*. You store your products at one of Amazon's fulfillment centers; they pick, pack, ship, and provide cus-tomer service for you. It has created a whole new category of business known as Amazon FBA or Fulfillment by Amazon.

Sell Your Knowledge Online

Learn how to package your knowledge and experience to generate income online. You can use your expertise to write e-books and generate extra income on Amazon.

Packaging your expertise into informational recordings can be a source of income. One person sold instructions how to build a potato gun by shooting a potato through a PVC pipe. He reportedly made $250,000 from people purchasing the instructions.[85]

Have skills as a business assistant? Start earning money as a virtual assistant on websites like VA Networking, People Per Hour, or Upwork.com. Are you a photographer? Create and sell images online at 500px Prime, SmugMug Pro, or iStock. Are you a video editor? Podcast editor? Have some other talent? Try offering it on *Fiverr.com*. Are you a talented seamstress? Set up a shop on etsy.com and sell wedding or holiday decorations, curtains, and pillows.

Complete online surveys, write articles for websites, or offer your social media skills for entrepreneurs on Facebook, Twitter, or Instagram. Help them promote their businesses, get more reviews, and find new customers.

Are you an inventor? Raise money on *kickstarter.com* to produce your invention. Get creative and motivated about how to generate additional income. Look for new ideas online. What skills do you have that could help you make extra money?

Making money with an online blog is certainly possible by offering products as an affiliate and being paid a commission on what you sell. Young girls are teaching how to apply makeup on YouTube channels and are making millions of dollars. Some are even able to parlay their popularity into their own products, such as a private label makeup brand.

Kylie Jenner is a name familiar to most people, but they may not realize she has parlayed her fame into a $400 million cosmetics company using social media like Instagram and YouTube.[86] That means her advertising has been free. You do not have to be a Kardashian to make it big in cosmetics. Unknown young women are becoming online celebrities by teaching makeup tutorials and then creating their own product lines like Jenner did. Michelle Phan earns $3 million annually from advertising revenues on her channel, endorsements, commissions, and her own makeup line.[87]

Or take the case of a twenty-three-year-old former waitress who quit her job and had no prospects for work. Her sister had a beauty channel on YouTube, so she decided to start her own channel on crafting. Eventually it became a sensation with over six million subscribers. She teaches how to make a green slime called Gak and makes six figures a month by recording and uploading three videos a week. Recently she even bought a house. [88]

Think Rental Income

Rent out a room in your home. With Airbnb, you can rent out a room in your home and generate extra income. Do you have sporting events, concerts, or conferences coming to a city near you? Those are great times to rent out a room. If you live in an area that is an in-demand vacation destination, you could also list your home on Vacation Rental by Owner (*VRBO.com*). One woman owns a second home and rents it out on VRBO for extra income and earns $33,000 a year.

Look for other assets you have to rent. One woman I know rents out her recreational vehicle for $150–$300 a night on *RVShare.com* and makes thousands of extra dollars per month. Do what you can to use what you have to generate extra income and then invest it.

Understand Social Security

There is a lot of debate about whether to take your Social Security early or wait until later. The benefit increases if you start later, so how can you tell what the right decision is?

You can collect benefits starting at age sixty-two, but your benefits will be reduced by 25 percent or 30 percent if you were born after 1960. The retirement age is sixty-six if you were born between 1943 and 1954, and the age rises if you were born later. If you can wait until age seventy, you will receive the most income. You receive the benefit for as long as you live, so extra years with larger checks can make a difference.

If you are out of work or in dire straits, then start taking your Social Security benefit at age sixty-two, but beyond that, it is best to put it off as long as possible assuming you live a long life. If you are in good health and still working, wait until at least age sixty-six and, even better, if you can wait, until age seventy.

If you outlive your spouse, you will receive a survivor's benefit. If your spouse takes early benefits, you will continue to receive a reduced check after they are gone. Make sure your spouse waits until age sixty-six to start their benefits if possible, so after they pass away you aren't locked into a 25 percent lower income.

The soundness of the Social Security program is somewhat murky, but to shore up the system, further reductions of benefits have been proposed as well as raising the retirement age and, of course, increasing taxes. The government provides calculators for your benefits at *SSA.gov*.

Inspiring Examples of Late Financial Bloomers

Even if you are starting late and are close to retirement age, you have a Wealth Heiress inside of you. No matter what you are starting with, anything is possible if you put what you have learned into action. Here are a few women (and a couple of well-known men) who started later in life and had great success:

Fashion designer Vera Wang did not design her first dress until she was forty. Prior to that, she was a figure skater and journalist. Now she is well known for bridal fashion design and as one of the world's premier women designers.[89]

Robin Chase cofounded ZipCar, the world's largest car-sharing and car-club service, at age forty-two in 2000. She owned 1.3 percent after multiple rounds of funding, worth about $6.3 million after an acquisition worth $491 million. She left the company in 2011 and continues to advise start-ups.[90]

Julia Child wrote her first cookbook at age fifty-one, launching herself as a celebrity chef and TV personality introducing French cooking to America. Her net worth at the time she died was estimated to be $38 million.[91]

Grandma Moses, a self-taught artist, began painting at age seventy-eight. She became widely famous for her nostalgic paintings depicting rural American life. While she did not benefit directly because she died in 1961, one of her paintings sold for $1.2 million in 2006.[92]

Anne Scheiber retired from the IRS at age fifty-one and began buying stocks with $5,000. Five years later, she bought 1,000 shares of Schering-Plough Corp. for about $10,000. Through stock splits and over forty-five years, her shares became worth $7.5 million.[93]

There are some great examples of men who have also succeeded later in life. Sam Walton founded Walmart at age forty-four and went on to become a billionaire. Colonel Sanders founded Kentucky Fried Chicken at age sixty-two and sold it twelve years later for $2 million.[94]

These are but a few examples of people who took a chance later in life and had tremendous success. As a Wealth Heiress, your potential is within you, ready for you to access any time. It is up to you to make the leap.

Strategies around Compounding

In previous chapters, we have talked about risk and compounding. It is vital to understand that your Millionaire Action Plan (MAP)™ is a living plan. That means the strategies change. That is particularly important to understand when it comes to the compounding aspect of the money engines you select.

Stock market pullbacks and crashes are part of investing, so you need to have a strategy to handle them. Rather than hoping they will not happen, you have to accept them as part of investing and learn what to do because the stock market drops about 10 percent every eleven months on average. The Dow Jones Industrial Average has dropped 20 percent twelve times since the end of WWII. That is about every six years.

So why doesn't everyone know this? Why do we act like a sharp pullback is unusual? Rather than ignore it, let's embrace pullbacks and crashes. Like Warren Buffet says, the stock market is the only thing that, when it goes on sale, no one wants to buy it.[95]

Before I tell you what to do after a crash or pullback, let me make an important point. I want you to remember that non-growth is the enemy, not pullbacks and crashes. What I mean by that is *not investing and not growing your money* is worse than investing and experiencing a pullback or crash. You might not think so intuitively, but it is true. You are worse off in your 401(k) or your IRA by not investing in stocks than you are if there is a pullback or crash.

Why? Because by not investing, you will not get to compound at higher rates. You must compound at higher rates in order to build wealth. You cannot let your money sit in a money market account at one percent for thirty years and expect to become wealthy. Wealth is about investing. And to do that, you have to take risk. You have to invest. Whether it is stocks, real estate, silver, or whatever you choose to invest in, you have to take risk.

You can mitigate risk by studying cycles and understanding where the best place to invest is long term. So let's talk about how to embrace declines in the stock market and what to do when it happens.

1. **Do nothing.** That's right. When you experience a sharp pullback or a crash, it is too late. If you did not know from cycles that it was coming ahead of time and could raise cash before it happened, then it is too late to do it after the crash. In fact, selling after a crash is the worst thing you can do. Do not do it! Do not sell! Most of the time, the stock market will at least have a strong move upward after the crash. That is called a dead-cat bounce. So wait for the move up if you are considering selling. My advice is do not sell even after the dead-cat bounce. It may take a few months or a few years, but the stock market has always recovered eventually and then gone higher. It likely will next time too.

2. **Do not panic.** Do not call your broker and say, "Get me out! I do not care if I've lost money, just get me out!" Many inexperienced investors right at the very bottom speak those very words, before the big dead-cat bounce comes. What you have done is locked in your losses. You are not invested, so you

will not benefit from the bounce. You may fear you are going to lose all your money and guess what, your fear is going to cause it to happen if you sell at the bottom. Do not do it!

3. **Resist the urge to sell.** Under all conditions, resist the urge to sell. This is not the time to sell. You will only do yourself serious harm if you sell. Accept that pullbacks and crashes are part of stock market investing. Expect it. Embrace it. Relax and know it won't last forever, no matter what the pundits are saying and how many Chicken Littles appear on CNBC saying the world is ending. Remember the stock market is made up of businesses and businesses sell things to people. When you wake up tomorrow, you will still have to eat, work, drive, and buy things, and so will everyone else. You may change your spending priorities depending on how well the economy is doing, but you still will spend money. Therefore, companies will still be in business tomorrow even if their stock price is a lot lower today.

4. **Consider buying. Stocks are on sale.** Yesterday stocks were a lot more expensive than they are today, so decide if you want to buy. Think about the products and services you spend your money on. They may be a place to start looking for potential investments. What are the trends today that will continue for years? For example, are healthcare companies something that could have strong sales for years to come? Perhaps they are worthy of further investment research like are they overvalued or undervalued? What is their earnings growth rate? Is it sustainable? Is it steady? What is their relative strength compared to their competitors? Are insiders buying? These are just a few things to consider before investing.

5. **Consider rebalancing your portfolio.** After a crash or pullback, take a look at your portfolio and see if you are positioned as well as possible. Think about what percentage you have in large caps, mid-caps, small caps, bonds, international, emerging markets, real estate, precious metals and other mutual funds or ETFs. Perhaps you have too much in large company stocks and want to add in smaller companies that

are strong growers in a niche and can navigate tough waters in a recession better—like a speedboat versus a cruise ship?

6. **Check your fear level.** Fear does nothing but cause you to freeze, so if you are feeling fearful, start doing some research that will make you feel more empowered. Go buy an *Investor's Business Daily* and read it. See what they are saying and look at the charts of the market leaders. It is an inexpensive way to do professional research.

7. **Check your 401(K).** Go online and check out what your 401(k) is invested in. Large companies that pay dividends might be a good buy because you get the dividend plus stock appreciation. Together, they can provide a good return and compounding rate.

8. **Get your shopping list together.** Think about what stocks you've wanted to own the last few years. This might be the time to pick them up for a bargain. Be sure nothing has changed with them fundamentally. If they still are going to have strong sales and strong growth, consider buying them. Look at their chart. Look at their earnings and profit and earnings ratio. Are insiders buying? Are they doing a stock buyback where the company is purchasing their own stock?

9. **Look at dividend-paying stocks.** I've already mentioned why dividend-paying stocks can be a good idea because of the dividend plus the price appreciation. There is an ETF that invests in a minimum of forty companies with rising dividends for the last twenty-five years. It is called Dividend Aristocrats.[96] Consider adding it to your portfolio for solid companies with good track records of paying dividends.

10. **Think about buying defensive, consumer-staple–oriented companies.** Investopedia defines consumer staples as "goods that people are unable or unwilling to cut out of their budgets regardless of their financial situation. Consumer staples stocks are considered non-cyclical, meaning that they are always in demand, no matter how well the economy is performing."[97] Think about adding defensive companies to your portfolio—things people spend money on like cigarettes,

liquor, pharmaceuticals, groceries, dollar stores, liquidators, gas, drug stores, snacks, soft drinks, fast food, and cosmetics even if there's a recession. There are a variety of consumer staples ETFs to consider.[98]

What to Do If the Real-Estate Market Crashes

A lot of people experienced a bona fide real-estate crash when prices tumbled 23.4 percent in October 2008, according to a twenty-city Case-Shiller housing index composite. Some cities like Phoenix, Las Vegas, and San Francisco fell more than 30 percent on a year-over-year basis. In October alone, nearly 85,000 people lost their homes to foreclosure.[99]

What can you do during such volatile times? I am going to walk you through how to stay rational and consider your options. The first thing is: do not panic. Letting your emotions run away from you is never a place that you can make good decisions from. Stay calm and rational and look at your situation. How much did you pay for your home? What are houses like it selling for today? These are known as comps or comparable prices that similar homes are selling for. They are facts, not conjecture. If the home next door to you just sold for $350,000, and it is very similar size, square footage, age, and condition as yours, then your home is worth about the same.

Of course, if there is a big difference like it has the original thirty-year-old kitchen and baths and your home is all updated, then yours is worth $350,000 plus an additional amount for the upgrades. A buyer will likely pay more for a home they do not have to remodel and is turnkey ready to move into.

Now that you know approximately what your home is currently worth, how much do you owe? Are you underwater, meaning you owe more than it is worth? Do you want to walk away from all your equity? Is it worth ruining your credit? Sometimes, it is best to stay put rather than act hastily.

Robin bought a home at the peak of the market for $475,000. She invested an additional $100,000 for a pool, hot tub, patio, and cabana. The market crashed, and her $575,000 investment was now worth about $350,000, leaving her $225,000 in the hole. At first, she was going to walk away and let it go to foreclosure, so she stopped making payments. After looking around at where she could move to, she realized she'd have to pay about $1,500 to rent a new place, and it wouldn't nearly be as nice as her home. So she borrowed $10,000 from a friend and paid off the back payments, interest, and penalties, deciding to stay in her home.

Over time she paid off her friend and made extra principal payments on her mortgage to increase the equity in her home and pay down the debt faster. Ten years later, her home is worth about $450,000, but she only owes $215,000, so she still has her lovely home, a nice amount of equity, and has maintained her good credit.

Ann lived in New York and bought a second home in Florida. She paid $600,000 right at the peak of the market. She was still working and did not have much vacation time, so she rented her Florida house on a seasonal basis, getting $4,000 a month for nine months each year. That brought her rental income of $36,000 for three years or a total of $108,000. When prices dropped and her home was worth $500,000, she did not worry because her cost basis had been effectively reduced by $108,000 because of the rental income. She did not panic because she realized she was about breaking even.

Samantha also bought a second home, a lovely condo on a golf course in Arizona. She paid $475,000 and spent about $50,000 remodeling the bathrooms, kitchen cabinets, appliances, and flooring. A few years later, another unit nearby was sold out of foreclosure for $360,000. She panicked because she still owed $370,000 on her home. She realized if she sold it she would possibly have to pay out of her pocket. What could she do? Taking a lesson from Ann, she rented her condo seasonally, bringing in $3,600 a month. She also paid $200 extra principal each month on her mortgage to pay down her loan faster and increase the equity. She will quickly be in a better financial position and out of the hole if she needs to sell soon.

Strategies like refinancing to a lower fixed interest rate, paying extra principal, and renting out a room or the whole house are helpful ideas that can help you improve a bad situation. Of course, your situation may be different and more dire.

If so, contact your bank about a possible short sale. A short sale, also known as a pre-foreclosure, is selling your home for less than the balance on the mortgage. If the mortgage company agrees to it, you can pay off some or all of your mortgage with the proceeds. It is a last resort, but the option may be available to you.

I'm sure there are more strategies available to you depending on your specific situation, so check with your bank and a real-estate agent if you find yourself in a bind. These are just a few strategies that have worked and may help you avoid a disaster.

The Bottom Line

Your Millionaire Action Plan (MAP)™ is an evolving process. Do not feel discouraged if your plan seems insurmountable to accomplish. As you make progress in one area, whether money (M), compounding (c), or time (T), it is going to improve your entire picture. If you are lacking in one part of the wealth-building (McT) formula, make up for it in other parts of the formula.

No matter what you invest in, wild price swings and possible crashes will likely happen. They are a part of investing and outside of your control. Usually the best strategy is to keep a long-term view and not get caught up in the fear. Over time, rational heads prevail, and often investments will go on to exceed the old highs and create new ones. Hang in there, stay calm, and consider your options.

Activate Your Wealth Heiress

1. Create your Millionaire Action Plan (MAP)™ today. It is important for you to have a plan.
2. What are your strengths and weaknesses? Learn to build on your strengths rather than improving weaknesses.
3. Each year when you calculate your net worth, revise your MAP™.

CHAPTER 20

Now Go Do It!

*"Get started, take action, and believe with
certainty you will achieve your goals."*

By now you realize mistakes you may have made with your wealth building. The light bulb may have gone on and you realize where you fell short. Or you may be patting yourself on the back that you've done a good job. I hope it is the latter, but unfortunately that won't be true for many women.

Hopefully, you see it is not too late—no matter how old you are, how little you've saved, or how much you may have avoided financial matters. Now you know that your Wealth Heiress exists, and she is ready, willing, and able to get you to your desired destination. You just need to take action and course-correct when you get off track. No one is perfect, so it will happen, but as long as you keep going, I am *certain* you will succeed.

Women are such hard workers and do so much for other people without being asked. It might feel like it is overwhelming to put one more thing on your plate. I understand completely. You are exhausted with taking care of everyone else, and now you have to take care of the investing too?

Actually, no. Remember when we talked about how investing is a lot of checking in while your investments are baking (compounding)? How the work is up-front like when you are cooking, but most of the time is spent letting it cook in the oven?

Once you have invested in your money engine of stocks or real estate or other investments, you are going to watch them. You will periodically meet with your partner or your financial advisor to review the portfolio. There is not a whole lot of fussing that is needed.

Looking at Cycles Going Forward

We talked about cycles and how cycles change. Be aware we have been in a low interest rate, low inflation environment, and it is about a thirty- to thirty-five-year cycle, peak to trough. Interest rates peaked in 1980 when the Federal Funds rate hit 20 percent[100] and bottomed in July 2015.[101]

If you are investing for the next thirty years, think about things that are inexpensive today that might be worth more in the future. For example, I think silver coins are a bargain today. I encourage all of my clients to buy them and have some coins in their possession. In 1980, silver peaked at $49.45 per ounce, and now thirty years later, it is only $16 per ounce.

What else can you buy that costs less than it did thirty years ago? A local coin dealer in the closest major city or an online dealer can get you American Eagle silver dollars, or if you live outside of the U.S., get your country's silver dollars. I like gold coins too, but they are much more expensive per ounce, so percentage-wise silver should appreciate more. Having up to 10 percent in a portfolio might be a good long-term strategy.

As we move toward higher inflation over the next thirty years, real assets like land, farms, precious metals, and collectibles like fine art, rare cars, old coins, baseball cards, and stamps may come back into favor. You can pick up some of these things today very inexpensively. What you've learned in this book about bubbles and cycles is literally at the level you could converse with billionaires. You've got knowledge that has been kept closely guarded by a small group. That, along with business cycles, should help give you a framework that will help you invest.

Putting It All Together

We've covered a lot of ground, and I've shown you some treacherous traps that keep you from achieving your goals. I hope you embrace opportunity cost and start seeing it in everything you buy. Things like celebrity closet syndrome are seductive and keep women from achieving real wealth by only providing an illusion of wealth.

I want you to be the empowered, self-confident Wealth Heiress you are, not an imitation of one. It is important to invest and compound money for your future, rather than having racks and shelves packed with expensive things displayed in a closet like a museum collection. Once you've made your millions, then you can add more to your collection, but you can wear only one at a time anyway, so why not pare back and just have a couple expensive handbags and put the money saved into some good ETFs, mutual funds, or stocks?

The Most Valuable Thing on Earth

The most valuable thing on Earth is time. You live each moment only once, and then it is gone. You cannot buy additional time, and no one knows how much he or she has. People who are wealthy know this and often trade their wealth to have more time. They hire people to do tasks for them so they can enjoy more time with friends and family. They do not have to go to a job, so they have more free time to pursue hobbies. No matter how much you are paid at your job or in your business, I want you to start thinking of your time like a millionaire does. I want you to realize how much it is really worth.

If you made $1 million a year at a job, had two weeks' vacation, and worked forty hours per week, do you know how much your hourly rate would be? Let's calculate it. Fifty weeks times forty hours is 2,000 hours. A million dollars divided by 2,000 is $500 per hour. Therefore, if you earned a million dollars a year, your time would be worth $500 per hour.

Now that you know how valuable your time really is, does that change your perspective? The average American watches five hours of television a day.[102] That is $2,500 a day down the drain!

Here's an idea for you. Take half of that time, and use it to become more knowledgeable about investing. A lot of women tell me they listen to the *Be Wealthy & Smart* podcast while they are driving to work, walking the dog, or folding the laundry.

I listen to YouTube videos of financial interviews while I put my makeup on in the morning. I often listen to a business podcast while I am having breakfast or driving to the grocery store. On Saturdays, I get *Investor's Business Daily* (IBD) delivered. It takes about only fifteen minutes to scan the information I need from it. I review some charts and see if there are pertinent articles. I do not need to read it cover to cover. I listen to books on tape as much as reading physical or Kindle books.

A Final Message

I hope you've already started to connect with your Wealth Heiress by putting a plan into action. It is up to you whether you follow through on building wealth and reaching your goals.

This is my hope for you: You will have taken action on the Six Steps to Wealth, the Wealth Building Formula™, and your Millionaire Action Plan (MAP)™, exceeding your goals and realizing your Wealth Heiress. How the story turns out is up to you. I hope you decide to step up and grab the brass ring. Your Wealth Heiress is waiting for you, and I'm here to help you every step of the way.

The Bottom Line

There are no coincidences. You found this book for a reason. It is a tap on the shoulder for you to get your finances in order and advance the path of realizing your Wealth Heiress. Only you can decide to do it. You must be involved, even if someone else is handling your investments. Take the time to understand what you are investing in and why, how it is compounding for you, and what you want to add to your portfolio because of cycles. Be proactive and assertive. There is no time like the present.

Activate Your Wealth Heiress

Now that you've read this book, review it over and over. Visit my website, *wealthheiress.com*, and see the support services available for your continued learning and success. Further your learning by listening to the *Be Wealthy & Smart* podcast. Get more tips and inspiration by connecting with me on social media. Get your free resources and calculator on my website. Remember to talk with your partner, financial advisor, and gather a team of professionals.

Your Wealth Heiress Checklist

Here is the Wealth Heiress checklist of things to put into practice:

1. Create your MAP™ and your strategy to overcome your shortcomings with McT.
2. Pay off debt except your mortgage.
3. Pay 1/12 extra per month on your mortgage.
4. Create your five clear spending priorities.
5. Decide what you do not value and will stop spending money on.
6. Calculate your net worth annually.
7. Stop buying depreciating assets.
8. Add appreciating assets to your net worth.
9. Max out your 401(k).
10. Create a will, advanced directive, and power of attorney.*
11. Consider a revocable living trust for out-of-state property.*
12. Talk to an attorney about estate planning if you have substantial assets.*
13. If your estate is worth over a million, see an attorney.*
14. Review your insurance coverage.
15. Write your affirmations and say them daily.
16. Contribute to charity or start a Donor Advised Fund.
17. Save 20 percent.
18. Read financial books and publications.
19. Write regularly in your Wealth Heiress journal.

20. Go to my website at *wealthheiress.com* for updates and calculators.
21. Listen to the *Be Wealthy & Smart* podcast.
22. Connect with me on social media. See Resources at the end of this book.
23. Have regular financial meetings at least quarterly with your spouse or partner.
24. Look into starting a side hustle or online business.
25. Clean out your closet.
26. Review your investment statements monthly.

*I'm not a lawyer, so please seek counsel regarding the laws in your state.

Resources

Resources mentioned in the book can be found on my website, including the financial calculator, my list of favorite financial books, *Be Wealthy & Smart* podcasts, debt spreadsheets, affirmations, and more.

Websites

Get free additional resources at*: wealthheiress.com.*

Connect with Me on Social Media

If you enjoyed the book, please post a photo of yourself with the Wealth Heiress book on Instagram or Facebook and use **#WealthHeiressBook.**

I love creativity or humor with the photos. Follow me and tag me on Instagram @lindapjones or Facebook @lindapjonesfanpage. I'll select photos to feature on my page. I want to see *you* there!

Connect with me on social media for more wealth tips:

Facebook: *https://www.facebook.com/LindaPJonesFanPage*

Twitter: *https://twitter.com/LindaPJones*

Instagram: *https://www.instagram.com/lindapjones*

LinkedIn: *https://www.linkedin.com/in/lindapjones*

GooglePlus: *https://plus.google.com/+LindaPJones*

Pinterest: *https://www.pinterest.com/lindapjonesAWM*

Podcast (Online Radio Show)

Free wealth mentoring is available by listening to the *Be Wealthy & Smart* Podcast: *lindapjones.com/itunes*

Shop

Shop Wealth Heiress products at *wealthheiress.com/shop*.

ENDNOTES

1   Jackie Augustine, "Research Brief: Women Control $20 Trillion in Annual Consumer Spending," The Imaging Alliance, September 10, 2015. https://www.theimagingalliance.com/research-brief-women-control-20-trillion-in-annual-consumer-spending/

2   "Statistics on the Purchasing Power of Women," *Girlpower Marketing*, 2017. https://girlpowermarketing.com/statistics-purchasing-power-women/

3   Chris Taylor, "Why Women Are Better Investors: Study," *Reuters*, June 7, 2017. https://www.reuters.com/article/us-money-investing-women/why-women-are-better-investors-study-idUSKBN18Y2D7

4   Stacy Torres, "Aging Women, Living Poorer," *Contexts*, May 21, 2014. https://contexts.org/articles/aging-women-living-poorer/

5   "Benjamin Disraeli on Greatest Riches," *Made of Money*, July 25, 2013. http://itsamoneything.com/money/benjamin-disraeli-quote-share-riches-reveal/#.WjLwoFQ-fYI

6   "The Most Successful Dividend Investors of All Time," *Dividend Growth Investor*, February 16, 2017. http://www.dividendgrowthinvestor.com/2017/02/the-most-successful-dividend-investors.html

7   Ibid.

8   James K. Glassman, "An Old Lady's Lesson: Patience Usually Pays," *The Washington Post*, December 17, 1995, https://www.washingtonpost.com/archive/business/1995/12/17/an-old-ladys-lesson-patience-usually-pays/ec000053-d7bf-4014-b841-546bd5847a80/

9   John Waggoner, "First Woman Member of the NYSE Siebert Dies at 80," *USA Today*, August 25. https://www.usatoday.com/story/money/business/2013/08/25/muriel-siebert-dies/2697957/

10 "Sara Blakely Quotes," *BrainyQuote*, https://www.brainyquote.com/quotes/sara_blakely_421768

11 "How Spanx Got Started," *Inc.*, June 5, 2017, https://www.inc.com/sara-blakely/how-sara-blakley-started-spanx.html

12 Robert Frank, "Billionaire Sara Blakely Says Secret to Success Is Failure," CNBC, October 16, 2013, https://www.cnbc.com/2013/10/16/billionaire-sara-blakely-says-secret-to-success-is-failure.html

13 Jennifer Lopez, "Doubt is a killer. You just have to know who you are and what you stand for," *BrainyQuote*. https://www.brainyquote.com/quotes/jennifer_lopez_460714

14 Allison Hache, "Jennifer Lopez's Net Worth Is $360 Million," *Bankrate*, April 24, 2017, http://www.bankrate.com/lifestyle/celebrity-money/jennifer-lopez-net-worth/

15 "J. K. Rowling Biography.com," *The Biography.com website*, last modified December 15, 2017. https://www.biography.com/people/jk-rowling-40998

16 "Debbi Fields Quotes," *BrainyQuote*, https://www.brainyquote.com/authors/debbi_fields

17 "Debbi Fields (Mrs. Fields Cookies)," *LocalWiki*, https://localwiki.org/oakland/Debbi_Fields_%28Mrs._Fields_Cookies%29; Katherine Michalak, "Debbi Fields: FACES of the South," *StyleBlueprint*, https://styleblueprint.com/everyday/debbi-fields-faces/

18 "Oprah Winfrey > Quotes > Quotable Quote." *goodreads*, https://www.goodreads.com/quotes/625783-create-the-highest-grandest-vision-possible-for-your-life-because

19 J. J. Mccorvey, "The Key To Oprah Winfrey's Success: Radical Focus," *Fast Company*, October 12, 2015. https://www.fastcompany.com/3051589/the-key-to-oprah-winfreys-success-radical-focus.

20 Rob Wile, "Meet the Wonderfully Nerdy CEO Who Is Now America's Richest Self-Made Woman in Tech," *Money*, June 30, 2017. http://time.com/money/4839017/judy-faulkner-billionaire-epic/

21 "Gabrielle 'Coco' Chanel," *Entrepreneur*, October 10, 2008. https://www.entrepreneur.com/article/197624#

22 Ibid.

23 "Arianna Huffington Quotes," *BrainyQuote*, https://www.brainy-quote.com/quotes/arianna_huffington_393656

24 "Arianna Huffington Biography.com," *The Biography.com website*, last modified August 11, 2016. https://www.biography.com/peo-ple/arianna-huffington-2121653n

25 "Zhou Qunfei Quotes," *BrainyQuote*, https://www.brainyquote.com/quotes/zhou_qunfei_875940; Ruth Umoh, "This Former Factory Worker Is Now the World's Richest Self-Made Wom-an," *CNBC*, July 17, 2017. https://www.cnbc.com/2017/07/17/meet-zhou-qunfei-the-worlds-richest-self-made-woman.html

26 John Rothchild, "When the Shoeshine Boys Talk Stocks It Was a Great Sell Signal in 1929. So What Are the Shoeshine Boys Talking about Now?" *archive.fortune.com*, April 15, 1996. http://archive.fortune.com/magazines/fortune/fortune_ar-chive/1996/04/15/211503/index.htm

27 Charles Nenner, "It's the Cycle, Stupid—Following Market Pat-terns," *Institutional Investor*, November 30, 2011. https://www.institutionalinvestor.com/article/b150zsr0nz9rfq/its-the-cy-cle-stupid-following-market-patterns

28 Ibid.

29 "David Gurwitz Interviews Charles Nenner," *David Gurwitz Organization.* http://davidgurwitz.com/david-gurwitz-inter-views-charles-nenner/; David Gurwitz, conversation with au-thor, 2006.

30 "Edward R. Dewey," *Wikipedia*, January 6, 2018. https://en.wiki-pedia.org/wiki/Edward_R._Dewey

31 Ray Tomes, "Edward R Dewey and the Case for Cycles," *Cycles Research Institute's Blog*, July 11, 2010. https://cyclesresearchinsti-tute.wordpress.com/2010/07/11/edward-r-dewey-and-the-case-for-cycles/

32 Edward R. Dewey and Og Mandino, *Cycles: The Mysterious Forces That Trigger Events* (Manor Books, 1973), 15.

33   Nikola Tesla, "If you want to find the secrets of the universe, think in terms of energy, frequency and vibration," *Goodreads*. https://www.goodreads.com/quotes/361785-if-you-want-to-find-the-secrets-of-the-universe

34   "William Delbert Gann," *Cycles Research Institute*. http://cycles-researchinstitute.org/cycles-research/markets/w-d-gann/

35   "WD Gann Patient Studies Finally Paid Huge Rewards," *Brainyforex*. http://www.brainyforex.com/gann.html

36   Martin A. Armstrong, "The Business Cycle and the Future," *Armstrong Economics*, September 26, 1999. https://www.armstrongeconomics.com/writings/1999-2/the-business-cycle-and-the-future/

37   Edward R. Dewey and Og Mandino, *Cycles: The Mysterious Forces That Trigger Events* (Manor Books, 1973), 120.

38   "Paul Tudor Jones," *forex.info*, August 18, 2016. http://forex.info/paul-tudor-jones/

39   Bernard Baruch, "Talk:Bernard Baruch," *Wikiquote*, July 7, 2016. https://en.wikiquote.org/wiki/Talk:Bernard_Baruch

40   "Who's the Better Investor: Men or Women?" *Fidelity*, May 18, 2017, https://www.fidelity.com/about-fidelity/individual-investing/better-investor-men-or-womens

41   "Albert Einstein Famously Stated: 'Compound Interest Is the Eighth Wonder of the World. He Who Understands It, Earns It... He Who Doesn't... Pays It.' How Can the Average Person Use This?" *Quora*. https://www.quora.com/Albert-Einstein-famously-stated-"Compound-interest-is-the-eighth-wonder-of-the-world-He-who-understands-it-earns-it-he-who-doesn't-pays-it-"-How-can-the-average-person-use-this.

42   "107 Profound Warren Buffett Quotes: Learn to Build Wealth," *Sure Dividend*. https://www.suredividend.com/warren-buffett-quotes/

43   Alert Investor, "3 Things to Know about Dollar-Cost Averaging," *The Motley Fool*, October 27, 2016. https://www.fool.com/investing/2016/10/27/3-things-to-know-about-dollar-cost-averaging.aspx

44 "What Has Been the Annual Return on Google's Stock?" *Quora*. https://www.quora.com/What-has-been-the-annual-return-on-Googles-stock

45 Dan Caplinger, "Roth IRA Contribution Limits in 2018 -- and How to Work Around Them." *The Motley Fool*, December 2, 2017, https://www.fool.com/retirement/iras/2017/12/02/roth-ira-contribution-limits-in-2018-and-how-to-wo.aspxx

46 Pascal Bedard, "The Demographics of Stock Market Returns Part II," *Medium*, August 28, 2017. https://medium.com/street-smart/the-demographics-of-stock-market-returns-part-ii-a41a46622198

47 Napoleon Hill, *Think and Grow Rich* (Ballantine Books, 1960), 1.

48 Ibid., 14.

49 "Protect Your Wealth and Diversify Investments," *The Irish Times*, January 12, 2008. https://www.irishtimes.com/sponsored/private-wealth-management/protect-your-wealth-and diversify-investments-1.2355582

50 Jim Rohn, "You are the average of the five people you spend the most time with," *Goodreads*. https://www.goodreads.com/quotes/1798-you-are-the-average-of-the-five-people-you-spend

51 Thomas Stanley, *The Millionaire Next Door* (Longstreet Press, 1996), 47.

52 Oprah Winfrey, "Be thankful for what you have; you'll end up having more. If you concentrate on what you don't have, you will never, ever have enough," *BrainyQuote*. https://www.brainyquote.com/quotes/oprah_winfrey_163087

53 Ralph Waldo Emerson, "Once you make a decision, the universe conspires to make it happen," *BrainyQuote*. https://www.brainyquote.com/quotes/ralph_waldo_emerson_383633

54 "30 of Muhammad Ali's best quotes," *USA Today Sports*, last modified June 5, 2016." https://www.usatoday.com/story/sports/boxing/2016/06/03/muhammad-ali-best-quotes-boxing/85370850/

55 "The Ultimate Driving Campaign," *BMW Style TV*. http://www.bmwstyle.tv/the-ultimate-driving-campaign/

56 Napoleon Hill, "Think and Grow Rich—Chapter 3," *Genius*. https://genius.com/Napoleon-hill-think-and-grow-rich-chapter-3-annotated

57 *"Vibrational Frequency and the Subtle Energy Nature of Essential Oils,"* *BioSpiritual Energy Healing*. http://www.biospiritual-energy-healing.com/vibrational-frequency.html

58 Napoleon Hill, *Think and Grow Rich* (Ballantine Books, 1960), 74

59 Ester Bloom, "15 Years Later, 'Sex and the City' Writer Defends Carrie's Controversial Money Choices," *CNBC*, October 16, 2017. https://www.cnbc.com/2017/10/13/sex-and-the-city-writer-amy-harris-defends-how-carrie-handles-money.html

60 "Auntie Mame Quotes," IMDb. http://www.imdb.com/title/tt0051383/quotes

61 Mohit Tater, "These Bootstrapped Businesses Used Credit Cards for Startup Capital," *Entrepreneurship Life*, September 10, 2015. https://www.entrepreneurshiplife.com/bootstrapped-businesses-credit-cards-startup-capital/

62 "College Graduates Earn 84% More Than High School Grads, Study Says," *Los Angeles Times*, August 5, 2011. http://latimesblogs.latimes.com/money_co/2011/08/college-gradutates-pay.html

63 Tara Parker-Pope, "This Is Your Brain at the Mall: Why Shopping Makes You Feel So Good," *The Wall Street Journal*, December 6, 2005. https://www.wsj.com/articles/SB113382650575214543

64 "Nucleus Accumbens," Wikipedia, last modified December 23, 2017. https://en.wikipedia.org/wiki/Nucleus_accumbens

65 Warren Buffet, "The most important investment you can make is in yourself," *Goodreads*. https://www.goodreads.com/quotes/5205902-the-most-important-investment-you-can-make-is-in-yourself

66 "Inc. 5000 2017: The Full List," *Inc.* https://www.inc.com/inc5000/list/2017

67 "About," *P.F. Candle Co.* https://pfcandleco.com/pages/about

68 Burt Helm, "How This Mother of a Newborn Launched a $13 Million Business," *Inc.* https://www.inc.com/magazine/201709/burt-helm/2017-inc5000-lauren-james-enterprises.html

69 Kimberly Weisul, "How an Accountant Turned a Water Bottle Company into a $100 Million Fashion Brand," *Inc.* https://www.inc.com/magazine/201706/kimberly-weisul/swell-water-bottle-design-awards-2017.html

70 Andrew Carnegie, "The way to become rich is to put all your eggs in one basket and then watch that basket," *BrainyQuote.* https://www.brainyquote.com/quotes/andrew_carnegie_156212

71 "Albert Einstein—Compound Interest," *Quotes on Finance.* https://quotesonfinance.com/quote/79/Albert-Einstein-Compound-interest

72 Mark O. Haroldsen, *How to Wake Up the Financial Genius Inside You* (Marko Enterprises, 1977), 1.

73 Megan Leonhardt, "4 Things You Should Know Before You Make Your Own Will," *Money*, August 17, 2016. http://time.com/money/4443349/do-it-yourself-will/

74 "Unmarried Partners, Medical Directives and the Durable Power of Attorney for Finances," FindLaw. http://family.findlaw.com/living-together/unmarried-partners-medical-directives-and-the-durable-power-of.html

75 "Women Still Do More Household Chores Than Men, ONS Finds," *BBC*, November 10, 2016. http://www.bbc.com/news/uk-37941191

76 Kate Stalter, "Men Die Married, Women Die Single…" *Better Financial Decisions*, November 27, 2017. https://betterfinancialdecisions.com/men-die-married-women-die-single/

77 "Women 80% More Likely to Be Impoverished in Retirement," *National Institute on Retirement Security*, March 1, 2016. http://www.nirsonline.org/index.php?option=content&task=view&id=913

78 SpectrumGroup. https://spectrem.com

79 Ibid.

80 Farnoosh Torabi, "7 Financial Talks to Have with Your Partner to Keep from Arguing about Money," *Business Insider*, March 6, 2015. http://www.businessinsider.com/7-financial-talks-to-have-with-your-partner-to-keep-from-arguing-about-money-2015-3

81 "Calculators: Life Expectancy," *Social Security Administration.* https://www.ssa.gov/planners/lifeexpectancy.html

82 "What Is the Maximum I Can Receive from My Social Security Retirement Benefit?" *Investopedia*. https://www.investopedia.com/ask/answers/102814/what-maximum-i-can-receive-my-social-security-retirement-benefit.asp

83 Warren Buffet, "Do not save what is left after spending, but spend what is left after saving," *AZ Quotes*. http://www.azquotes.com/quote/689479

84 "These Side Hustles Can Pay $100,000 a Year," *MarketWatch*, December 28, 2017. https://www.marketwatch.com/story/how-to-earn-100000-or-more-with-side-hustles-2017-07-13

85 Grant Cardone, "Russell Brunson: From Wrestler to Marketing Genius," *Medium*, March 15, 2017. https://medium.com/@grantcardone/russell-brunson-from-wrestler-to-marketing-genius-9c9f626096e4

86 "Kylie Jenner Lip Kit's Worth over $400 Million!!! (If You Believe Kris Jenner)," *TMZ*, August 9, 2017. http://www.tmz.com/2017/08/09/kylie-jenner-lip-kit-billion-dollar-brand-kris-jenner/

87 Kathryn Kite, "How Michelle Phan Built a $500 Million Beauty Empire," *Yahoo!* July 12, 2016. https://www.yahoo.com/news/how-michelle-phan-built-a-500-million-beauty-203535337.html

88 Valerie Siebert, "YouTube Star Who Makes 'Slime' Videos Buys a Six-Bedroom House with Her Earnings, Revealing That She Makes Six Figures PER MONTH Creating the Goo," *Daily Mail*, June 25, 2017. http://www.dailymail.co.uk/femail/article-4637732/YouTube-star-makes-slime-videos-buys-six-bedroom-house.html

89 Richard Feloni, "24 People Who Became Highly Successful After Age 40," *Business Insider*, June 23, 2015. http://www.businessinsider.com/24-people-who-became-highly-successful-after-age-40-2015-6/#nald-fisher-was-40-and-had-no-experience-in-retail-when-he-and-his-wife-doris-opened-the-first-gap-store-in-san-francisco-in-1969-the-gaps-clothes-quickly-became-fashionable-and-today-the-company-is-one-of-the-worlds-largest-clothing-chains-2

90 Dinah Eng, "Robin Chase: Zipcar's Founder Finds a New Gear," *Fortune*, December 4, 2012. http://fortune.com/2012/12/04/robin-chase-zipcars-founder-finds-a-new-gear/

91 "Julia Child Net Worth," *Celebrity Net Worth*. https://www.celebritynetworth.com/richest-celebrities/richest-celebrity-chefs/julia-child-net-worth/

92 Ben Lewis, "Grandma Moses—a New Career in Her 80s!" *Engage as You Age*, May 17, 2010. http://engageasyouage.com/2010/05/17/grandma-moses-a-new-career-in-her-80s/

93 James K. Glassman, "An Old Lady's Lesson: Patience Usually Pays," *The Washington Post*, December 17, 1995. https://www.washingtonpost.com/archive/business/1995/12/17/an-old-ladys-lesson-patience-usually-pays/ec000053-d7bf-4014-b841-546bd5847a80/?utm_term=.327aa52a37c4

94 Chris Plante, "The Real Story of Colonel Sanders Is Far Crazier Than This Bland Inspirational Meme," *The Verge*, July 5, 2016. https://www.theverge.com/2016/7/5/12096466/colonel-sanders-kfc-meme-life-story

95 "107 Profound Warren Buffett Quotes: Learn to Build Wealth," *Sure Dividend*. https://www.suredividend.com/warren-buffett-quotes/

96 "S&P 500 Dividend Aristocrats ETF," *ProShares*. http://www.proshares.com/funds/nobl_index.html

97 "Consumer Staples," *Investopedia*. https://www.investopedia.com/terms/c/consumerstaples.asp

98 "Consumer Staples Equities ETFs," *ETFdb.com*. http://etfdb.com/etfdb-category/consumer-staples-equities/

99 Les Christie, "Home Prices Post Record 18% Drop," *CNNMoney.com*, December 30, 2008. http://money.cnn.com/2008/12/30/real_estate/October_Case_Shiller/index.htm?postversion=2008123014

100 "What Led to the High Interest Rates of the 1980s?" *PBS NewsHour*, May 29, 2009. https://www.pbs.org/newshour/economy/what-led-to-the-high-interest

101 "Have we seen interest rates bottom out?" *JCRA*. https://jcra-group.com/seen-interest-rates-bottom/

102 David Hinckley, "Average American Watches 5 Hours of TV per Day, Report Shows," *Daily News*, March 5, 2014. http://www.nydailynews.com/life-style/average-american-watches-5-hours-tv-day-article-1.1711954

ACKNOWLEDGMENTS

There are so many people to thank. To the many mentors, coaches, and other people who have inspired me over the years, beginning with my parents, who showed me firsthand how to build wealth and inspired me to create my own. To my sister Marilyn, who is the most giving person I know and my best cheerleader. To Linda Ruggles, who asked me to write this book years ago. To lifelong friends who believed in me, like Barbara and Jake Lansche, Sharon Wada, Rosie Feeney, Moyra Van Nus, Kathy Stover, Jamie Collins, Thelma Putzel, Jaci and Dick Lindstrom, Melody Summers, Doug Holsclaw, and BJ Shamburger. Friends who are there with a smile like Garrett, Dennis and Susan, Kay, Pamela, Karen, Monty, Bill, Stu, Jeff, Rick and Neil, David, Claire, and Eli. Friends who encouraged me like Thelma, Kathy, Jamie, Phyllis, Beth, Keri, Sherie, Tracy, Kate, Anne, Caren, and Debbie. You ladies are amazing. To mentors like Lisa Sasevich, Ali Brown, Sheri Keys, Rachel Hanfling, Tamara Gold, and Selena Soo. Thank you for your wisdom. And my apologies if I've forgotten to mention you here!

To my sister Susan, brother-in-law Jim, and brothers Gary and Ned, and their spouses and families—Mom and Dad live on in you.

In the writing of this book, I have had to rely on the expertise of many. To Debra Englander and the crew at Post Hill Press, thank you for believing in me and publishing my work. To my agents Leticia Gomez and Raoul Davis, thank you for helping me to be "discovered." To Kathy Palokoff, my editor, who was beside me from proposal to final drafts, thank you for your diligence, support, inspiration, and hard work on this project.

To Nancy Kennedy, Jack Kemp, Tom Chronert, Doug Brown, Chris Lovenguth, Rene' Love, Marilyn Penitsch, Rick Morry, John Champion, and Melinda Hawkins, words cannot express what you did to help me after my husband died. I can never repay your kindness. I am forever indebted to you. Thank you.

To the MoneyTree Investing podcast crew of Miranda Marquit, Joe Saul-Sehy, Doug Goldstein, and Steve Stewart, thank you for weekly inspiration.

To Napoleon Hill, Venita Van Caspel, Suze Orman, David Bach, Robert G. Allen, Tony Robbins, and Mark O. Haroldsen, thank you for paving the way and allowing me to stand on the shoulders of giants.

Finally, to women everywhere who work tirelessly taking care of others without expecting anything in return. Thank you for doing what you do and giving of yourself every day. You inspire me and make the world a better place. This book is for you.

ABOUT THE AUTHOR

Linda P. Jones is America's Wealth Mentor™. Her award-winning pod-cast, *Be Wealthy & Smart*, is listened to in 181 countries and has over 1.5 million downloads. Linda shares wealth building secrets, tips, and knowledge that made her $2 million at age 39. She teaches that financial freedom is about making the right choices, and anyone can become wealthy, no matter how much or how little money they are starting with.